Sermons for the Seed Sower

Arranged by
Johnie Edwards and John Isaac Edwards

© 2015 One Stone Press – All rights reserved.

No part of this publication may be reproduced, stored in a retrieval system, or transmitted in any way by any means—electronic, mechanical, photocopy, recording, or otherwise—without the prior permission of the copyright holder, except as provided by USA copyright law.

Published by:
One Stone Press
979 Lovers Lane
Bowling Green, KY 42103

Printed in the United States of America

ISBN-10: 1-941422-10-1
ISBN-13: 978-1-941422-10-6

www.onestone.com

Contents

1. No Greater Joy 7
2. God's Use of Water 9
3. Three Reasons People Fall Away 11
4. What the Church Is Not 13
5. What We Must Not Love 15
6. What We Must Love 17
7. Preaching Needed Today 19
8. Where Are You Walking? 21
9. Who Told You That? 23
10. How the Bible Describes Itself 25
11. What the Word of God Is Like 27
12. For What Is Your Life? 29
13. The Blessings of God 31
14. The Things of God 33
15. What It Means to Preach Christ 35
16. And Satan Came Also Among Them 37
17. Who Am I? 40
18. Sabbath Keeping 43
19. Bible Works 45
20. What Can Be Done With the Scriptures? 47
21. These Are the Greatest 49
22. Unto God Be the Glory 51

23. By the Blood of Christ 53
24. Before and After Baptism. 55
25. A Good Soldier of Jesus Christ. 57
26. Great Things in the Book of Jonah. 59
27. Some Who Cannot Please God 61
28. What We Must Do With Truth. 63
29. What We Must Not Do With Truth 65
30. Precious Things in the Epistles of Peter 67
31. The Great Commission. 69
32. Happy Is the Man. 71
33. The Holy Scriptures 73
34. Some Things to Be Found in Christians. 75
35. Praying Positions 77
36. The Music Passages. 79
37. Living Below in This Old Sinful World 81
38. They That Were Ready 83
39. God's Law Concerning Marriage, Divorce and Remarriage 85
40. Bible Examples of Bountiful Giving. 87
41. Kinds of Worship 89
42. Saved Like Noah 91
43. The One Body. 93
44. When a Father Offered His Son. 95
45. Respect for the Word of God 97
46. Men Needed in the Church 99
47. What Happens When You're Baptized. 101
48. Things Men Sold 103
49. Old Testament Hospitality. 105
50. New Testament Hospitality 107
51. A Plumb Line. 109

52. Let Us Rise Up and Build. 112
53. Expressions of Obedience. 115
54. Heroic Faith 118
55. Soul Winning. 121
56. Why Stop the Chariot?. 124
57. Six Houses 126
58. Accessing God's Grace. 129
59. I Am Resolved 132
60. Some Things Jesus Did Not Do 134
61. Some Things Jesus Did. 137
62. What Paul Told the Ephesians About the Church. 140
63. What Paul Told the Colossians About Christ 143
64. Reading and Understanding the Bible 147
65. Is It Too Much for You?. 149
66. "I of _____". 152
67. Principles to Help Us Prevail 154
68. Learning from the Conquest of Jericho 157
69. What I Owe the Local Church 159
70. Going the Way of All the Earth. 163
71. Behold, He Cometh with Clouds. .166
72. There Shall Be a Resurrection. 168
73. Standing Before the Judgment Seat of Christ. 171
74. Why All the Confusion Concerning the Holy Spirit? 174
75. Hold Fast the Pattern 177
76. Ensamples Written for Our Admonition 179
77. Why So Many Churches?. 182
78. The Classic Parable Collection 184
79. Tell Your Children. 188
80. Consequences of Keeping the Law of Moses 190

81. What Is the Church of Christ? 194
82. When the Day of Pentecost Was Come 197
83. Six Things All Men Have 200
84. Preaching What We Practice 203
85. A Ribband of Blue. 206
86. Is the Seed Yet in the Barn?. 208
87. And They All Began to Make Excuse. 210
88. When I Left the World. 212
89. They Continued Stedfastly. 214
90. When God's People Gave Too Much 217
91. Believing a Lie. 219
92. Great Things in Acts Eight 221
93. Some Who Cannot Be Jesus' Disciple. 223
94. Small Things 225
95. Can Man Be Saved Without Doing Anything? 228
96. The Home at the Beginning 230
97. David's Temple Preparations. 233
98. Anna 236
99. This One Thing I Do. 239
100. People of the Book. 242

~ 1 ~
No Greater Joy
3 John 3-4

Introduction

1. The word "joy" is found in 162 Bible verses.

2. The word "joy" means "delight in, as one rejoices for gladness."

3. This sermon considers some occasions of spiritual joy.

Discussion

I. When brethren walk in truth:

    A. 3 John 4

    B. The word "children" refers to God's people.

    C. The truth is "God's word" (John 17:17).

    D. 2 John 6

II. When the gospel is obeyed:

    A. When the eunuch made the good confession: "I believe that Jesus Christ is the Son of God," and was "baptized; he went on his way rejoicing" (Acts 8:37-39).

    B. Have you had this occasion to rejoice?

III. When one is persecuted for righteousness' sake:

    A. Matthew 5:10-12

    B. Not all persecution is bad!

    C. 2 Timothy 3:12

    D. Church persecution brought about church growth (Acts 12:1-24).

      E. 1 Peter 4:15-16

IV. When the lost are found:

      A. Luke 15 is about the lost.

      B. Luke 15:7, 9, 24

      C. We need to rejoice at these times.

V. When the withdrawn return:

      A. One was withdrawn from (1 Corinthians 5).

      B. He returned and brethren were told to "forgive, comfort and love him" (2 Corinthians 2:7).

      C. There should be "rejoicing" when such returns (2 Corinthians 2:3).

VI. When others rejoice:

      A. Romans 12:15

      B. Instead of being jealous, when others have rejoicing occasions, we need to rejoice with them!

      C. 1 Corinthians 12:26

VII. When a name is written in heaven:

      A. Luke 10:17-20

      B. Revelation 20:12-15

Conclusion

1. Come just now obeying the gospel or be restored.

2. That there can be a time of joy!

~ 2 ~
God's Use of Water
1 Peter 3:20

Introduction

1. From the Eden Garden through the book of Revelation, God made use of water.
2. We study how, down through the ages, God used water to accomplish His purpose.

Discussion

I. In the Garden of Eden:

    A. Genesis 2:10

    B. Four rivers are mentioned (Genesis 2:11-14).

II. Feet Washing:

    A. Used as an act of hospitality

    B. Genesis 18:4

    C. John 13:4-10

    D. Foot washing was among "good works," not worship (1 Timothy 5:10).

III. Keep the ark afloat:

    A. 1 Peter 3:20

    B. Noah was saved by water as the flood waters "bare up the ark" (Genesis 7:17).

IV. Refresh the earth:

    A. Rain showers refresh the earth.

    B. Psalm 72:6

V. Salvation from the Egyptians:

    A. God used the Red Sea waters to save Israel.

    B. Exodus 14:13-31

    C. Hebrews 11:29

VI. Cleansed Naaman's leprosy:

    A. 2 Kings 5:1-14

    B. God used the Jordan River to rid Naaman of leprosy at his obedience!

VII. A cup of cold water:

    A. Matthew 10:42

    B. God notices the smallest of things.

VIII. The new birth:

    A. John 3:1-8

    B. The waters of baptism "wash away sin" (Acts 22:16; Titus 3:5; Acts 8:36-39).

Conclusion

1. Let the waters of baptism wash away your past sins, after faith, repentance and confession of your faith (Hebrews 11:6; Acts 17:30; Matthew 10:32; Mark 16:16).

2. Why not respond just now?

~ 3 ~
Three Reasons People Fall Away
Luke 8:13

Introduction

1. A reading and study of the parable of the sower will reveal three major reasons people fall away.
2. Read the parable (Luke 8:5-15).

Discussion

I. The devil takes away the word:

    A. The wayside people

    B. Luke 8:12

    C. Luke 8:5

    D. The devil knows that if the word is taken out of the heart, one will not believe and be saved (Romans 10:17; Hebrews 11:6).

    E. We must be aware of Satan's devices; they are many (2 Corinthians 2:11; 13-15; Ephesians 4:27; 1 Peter 5:8).

II. In time of temptation:

    A. The rocky soil

    B. Luke 8:6

    C. Having no root, believe for a while; in time of temptation fall away (Luke 8:13)

    D. We need to learn that God provides a way of escape from temptation if we will but take it (1 Corinthians 10:13).

    E. The three ways or avenues of temptation (1 John 2:15-17)

  F. James 1:13-15
III. Choked with cares, riches and life's pleasures
  A. Thorny soil individuals
  B. Luke 8:7
  C. Luke 8:14
  D. A failure to bring forth fruit will just not 'cut it' with the Lord. He expects His people to be fruit-bearing (John 15:1-8; Romans 6:22).
  E. We need to be a Moses (Hebrews 11:23-26)!

Conclusion

1. We need to be like the "good ground" people with "honest and good hearts" (Luke 8:8, 15).

2. What kind of "soil" are you? Show proof of your heart as you come obeying the gospel!

~ 4 ~
What the Church Is Not
1 Corinthians 12:14

Introduction

1. The church is not what many think.

2. By understanding what the church is not, we can better understand what the church is. The church is not:

Discussion

I. The meeting house:

   A. Acts 17:24

   B. The church is made up of "lively stones" (1 Peter 2:5).

   C. "Fear came upon the church" (Acts 5:11). Ever see a building afraid?

   D. The church has "ears" (Acts 11:22). Meeting houses have no ears!

II. A denomination:

   A. The New Testament church is neither Catholic, Jewish or Protestant; it is non-denominational. Denominations are churches started by men.

   B. The word denomination says there has been division (1 Corinthians 1:10).

   C. Matthew 16:18; Psalm 127:1

III. A political organization:

   A. John 18:36

B. There are things of "Caesar" and the "things that are God's (Matthew 22:21). There must be a separation of church and state (Romans 13:1-6).
IV. A social institution:
   A. Romans 14:17
   B. The church has not been charged with the work of providing recreation and entertainment for its members (1 Timothy 5:16).
   C. The church has a divine work (Ephesians 4:11-12).
V. One member:
   A. 1 Corinthians 12:14
   B. The body is the church (Colossians 1:18).
   C. Therefore the church is not one member, but many (1 Corinthians 12:20).
   D. So never say, "I am a church of Christ!" There is no such thing.
VI. A religious convenience center:
   A. The church does not exist merely to help families in marrying their young, burying their dead, and providing some occasional spiritual balm to accommodate an otherwise worldly disposition.
   B. The church is so important that it was in God's eternal purpose (Ephesians 3:10-11).

Conclusion

While the church is not many things, it is all the Scriptures teach it to be!

~ 5 ~
What We Must Not Love
1 John 2:15-17

Introduction

1. By knowing what we must not love, will help us understand what we must love.
2. In this lesson we want to examine some things we must not love.

Discussion

I. Sleep:
   A. Proverbs 20:13
   B. The wise man is not telling us to never sleep. He is telling us that one can spend all of time sleeping that he will come to poverty.
   C. Romans 13:11

II. No false oath:
   A. Zechariah 8:17
   B. Must always be true to your word.
   C. Ecclesiastes 5:4-5

III. The praise of men:
   A. Matthew 6:5
   B. John 12:42-43

IV. Money:
   A. 1 Timothy 6:10

   B. Money "is the root of all evil."

   C. Discuss what the love of money can do.

V. The world:

   A. 1 John 2:15-17

   B. Worldliness has robbed the church of its power.

   C. We must not be so in love with worldly things that it hinders our true love.

~ 6 ~
What We Must Love
1 John 5:3

Introduction

1. Not only must we not love some things, there are things that we must love.

2. From Genesis 27:4 through Revelation 3:19, the word "love" can be found 286 times in the King James translation of the Bible.

3. We are looking at some things we must love.

Discussion

I. God:

   A. Deuteronomy 10:12

   B. Joshua 22:5

   C. Matthew 22:37

II. God's law:

   A. Psalm 119:163

   B. Psalm 119:97

   C. Psalm 119 provides us with lots of reasons for loving God's law. Let's look at some of these reasons.

   D. Today, we live under "the law of Christ" (Galatians 6:2).

III. Our enemies:

   A. Matthew 5:44; Romans 12:20-21

   B. The best thing to do with an enemy is to love him and make a friend of him!

IV. Neighbor as thyself:

    A. Matthew 19:19; Galatians 5:14

    B. Remember Luke 10:25-37.

    C. Romans 13:10; Romans 15:2; Ephesians 4:25; James 2:8

V. One another:

    A. John 13:34-35

    B. 1 Thessalonians 3:12; 4:9; Galatians 5:13

VI. The withdrawn when they repent:

    A. 2 Corinthians 2:1-8

    B. Sometimes we have a bad attitude toward the one returning from his sins!

VII. Husbands, wives, children:

    A. Ephesians 5:25-33

    B. Titus 2:4

VIII. His appearing:

    A. The second coming of Christ

    B. 2 Timothy 4:8

Conclusion

Are you loving these things (John 14:15, 23)? Come just now and obey the Lord!

~ 7 ~
Preaching Needed Today
2 Timothy 4:2

Introduction

1. The Bible sets forth the kind of preaching needed today.
2. Paul instructed young Timothy (2 Timothy 4:1-5).

Discussion

I. Balanced preaching:
   A. Not all positive and not all negative—try starting your vehicle without both!
   B. 2 positive and 4 negative (Jeremiah 1:10)
   C. 2 negative and 1 positive (2 Timothy 4:2)
   D. Try starting your vehicle without a positive and a negative ground!

II. Cut-to-the-heart preaching:
   A. Acts 7:51-60
   B. Study context.

III. Reproving, rebuking and exhorting preaching:
   A. 2 Timothy 4:1-5
   B. Discuss each point.

IV. World-turning preaching:
   A. Acts 17:1-6
   B. We need this today!

V. Bold preaching:
   A. Philippians 1:14; Ephesians 6:19-20
   B. Acts 4:13; Acts 9:27
VI. Public and private preaching:
   A. Acts 20:17-20
   B. Takes both kinds.
VII. Heart-pricking preaching:
   A. Acts 2:22-37
   B. Only way to motivate people is to get to their hearts.
VIII. In-season and out-of-season preaching:
   A. 2 Timothy 4:2
   B. Never a time to let up. Preach when they like it and when they don't like it!
IX. Preaching which can be understood:
   A. Nehemiah 8:4-8
   B. Ephesians 5:17; 3:4
X. Preaching which demands obedience:
   A. Acts 2:37-41
   B. Have to ask for their obedience!

Conclusion

Let's get back to book, chapter and verse preaching!

~ 8 ~
Where Are You Walking?
Romans 6:3-4

Introduction

1. The Bible word "walk" is used to describe the whole round of activities of a Christian, including his moral conduct.
2. It is important that we walk in the right things.

Discussion

I. In newness of life:
   A. Following baptism
   B. Romans 6:3-4

II. By faith:
   A. 2 Corinthians 5:7
   B. Like those "faith heroes" in Hebrews 11. Note some.

III. In good works:
   A. Ephesians 2:10
   B. Responsibility of every individual Christian

IV. In love:
   A. Ephesians 5:1-2
   B. John 13:34-35

V. In truth:
   A. 2 John 4; 3 John 1-4
   B. What it means to walk in truth (John 17:17; John 8:32)

VI. In the old paths:

    A. Jeremiah 6:16

    B. Few want to do this!

VII. Together:

    A. Amos 3:3

    B. Must walk as one.

VIII. According to divine rules:

    A. Galatians 6:16; Philippians 3:16

    B. Many have thrown the rule book out the window!

IX. In the light:

    A. 1 John 1:6-7

    B. Psalm 119:105; 130

X. In Christ:

    A. Colossians 2:6

    B. "In Christ" is what it's all about (Galatians 3:27).

Conclusion

Checked your walking lately?

~ 9 ~
Who Told You That?
Genesis 3:8-12

Introduction

1. Read and discuss Genesis 3:8-12.
2. People have been told a lot of different things religiously. A good question to ask: Who told you that?

Discussion

I. That we are not under any law today:

    A. When it is pointed out that we are not under the law of Moses today, some jump to the false conclusion that we are under no law today!

    B. Galatians 6:2; 1 Corinthians 9:21; 2 Timothy 2:5; Philippians 3:16

II. That Paul taught it was wrong to marry:

    A. Paul was unmarried, as he chose to be (1 Corinthians 7:7-8). He had the right to marry (1 Corinthians 9:5).

    B. Why did Paul say these things? "Due to the present distress" (1 Corinthians 7:26). There was some issue at this time (Hebrews 13:4).

III. That Paul did not believe in being baptized:

    A. Because he said 1 Corinthians 1:14!

    B. Why did Paul say this (1 Corinthians 1:15)?

    C. A study of the context will help answer this (1 Corinthians 1:10-13).

D. Paul believed in, taught baptism and was baptized (Romans 6:3-4; Galatians 3:27; 1 Corinthians 12:13).

IV. That we already have eternal life:

   A. It is being taught that the moment one believes, he is saved and already has eternal life.

   B In hope (Mark 10:29-30; Titus 1:1-2), if one is in Christ (1 John 5:11), promise of eternal life (1 John 2:25), if faithful (Revelation 2:10)

V. That it is okay if God didn't tell us not to:

   A. This argument is used to justify a lot of unscriptural things like mechanical/instrumental music in worship!

   B. When God specifies, we can't generalize, as everything else is excluded. For example, when God told Noah to build the ark of gopher wood, it excluded every other kind of wood without God mentioning all the other woods (Genesis 6:14)!

VI. That one is saved before baptism:

   A. Many teach this.

   B. Mark 1:16:16; Acts 2:38; Acts 22:16; Romans 6:3-4; 1 Peter 3:21

Conclusion

Don't be misled (Matthew 15:14).

~ 10 ~
How the Bible Describes Itself
2 Timothy 3:16-17

Introduction

1. The Bible is the best describer of itself. Since God is the author of this divine volume, surely He knows best how to tell us what it is.

2. This study takes a look at biblical descriptions of the word of God.

Discussion

I. Scripture/scriptures:

   A. Means "a writing" and is applied to both the Old and New Testaments (Mark 12:10; Psalm 118:22-23).

   B. 2 Timothy 3:16-17

   C. Every study needs to begin with them (Romans 4:3; Galatians 4:30).

II. Word of God:

   A. Romans 10:17

   B. 1 Thessalonians 2:13

   C. Psalm 119 contains words of appreciation for God's word.

III. Law of:

   A. Some times the Bible is called "the law of God and the law of Moses" (Ezra 7:6; Psalm 9:17; Romans 7:22; Galatians 6:2).

   B. We are under law today.

IV. First and second:

   A. Hebrews 10:9-10

B. Jeremiah 31:31-34; Hebrews 8:8-13
V. Will/testament:
  A. Hebrews 10:9-10
  B. Hebrews 9:16-17
VI. Seed:
  A. Luke 8:5-15
  B. 1 Peter 1:23
  C. 1 Corinthians 4:15; James 1:18
VII. Gospel:
  A. Mark 1:1; Mark 16:15-16
  B. Romans 1:16; Ephesians 1:13; 1 Corinthians 15:1
VIII. Faith:
  A. Just one (Acts 13:7-12; Ephesians 4:1-6; Jude 3).
  B. The gospel and the faith are the same (Galatians 1:23; 2:2).

Conclusion

Have you obeyed God's word?

~ 11 ~
What the Word of God Is Like
Psalm 19:10

Introduction

1. As you open the book of God, you will encounter the word of God being likened to a number of things.
2. It is the design of this lesson to cause us to have greater appreciation for God's word. The word of God is like:

Discussion

I. Fire:

    A. Jeremiah 23:29

    B. Fire purifies (Psalm 12:6).

    C. So does God's word (1 Peter 1:22; 1 Timothy 5:22; James 4:8).

II. A hammer:

    A. Jeremiah 23:29

    B. Can prick the hardest of hearts

    C. Like the sermon did in Acts 2 (Acts 2:37)

III. Seed:

    A. Luke 8:11

    B. Study the parable of the sower (Luke 8:5-15).

IV. A sword:

    A. Ephesians 6:17

    B. Hebrews 4:12

    C. There is a need for learning how to use it in an effective way.
V. A light:
    A. Psalm 119:105; 130
    B. 1 John 1:7
VI. Honey and the honeycomb:
    A. Psalm 19:10
    B. Honey in the honeycomb is very sweet.
VII. Milk/meat:
    A. 1 Corinthians 3:2
    B. 1 Peter 2:2; Matthew 4:4
VIII. Spirit and life:
    A. John 6:63-68
    B. Study it (2 Timothy 2:15).

Conclusion

1. Hear, believe, repent, confess your faith and be baptized (Acts 18:8).
2. Come just now (2 Corinthians 6:2)!

~ 12 ~
For What Is Your Life?
James 4:14

Introduction

1. Reading text: James 4:13-15
2. This sermon makes for a good funeral sermon.
3. Or, it can be preached anytime.

Discussion

I. Life is the gift of God:

   A. Genesis 2:7

   B. Acts 17:28

II. Life is the target of the devil:

   A. Satan began his work in the Eden garden (Genesis 3:1-6).

   B. He is out to get you! So we must not be "ignorant of his devices" (2 Corinthians 2:11).

   C. 1 Peter 5:8

III. Life is the schoolroom of eternity:

   A. Our earthly life is the only place to prepare for eternity.

   B. Amos 4:12

   C. The story of the wise and foolish virgins (Matthew 25:1-13)

      1. Notice: those who were ready went in!

      2. We can prepare to meet God, and we will, by hearing His word (Matthew 17:5), believing (John 8:24), repenting of

our sins (Acts 17:30), confessing our faith that Jesus Christ is the Son of God (Matthew 10:32; Acts 8:37), being baptized (Mark 16:16; Acts 2:38), and then being added to the Lord's church (Acts 2:47; 1 Corinthians 12:13). Then be a faithful, steadfast Christian (1 Corinthians 15:58; Revelation 2:10).

IV. Life is short:

    A. At its longest, earth life is very brief.

        1. A vapour (James 4:14)

        2. Of few days (Job 14:1-2)

        3. Just a moment (2 Corinthians 4:17)

        4. Short (Psalm 89:47)

    B. Now is the only time we really have (2 Corinthians 6:2)!

V. Life must be according to God's will:

    A. James 4:15

    B. Jesus ordered His life this way (John 6:38; Hebrews 10:9; Luke 22:42).

Conclusion

Love your life and prepare it for eternity (1 Peter 3:10)!

~ 13 ~
The Blessings of God
Ephesians 1:3

Introduction

1. The blessings of God are of two kinds: physical and spiritual. The physical blessings are such things as the sunshine, the air we breathe, our homes, clothing and other such physical blessings (Matthew 5:45).

2. The spiritual blessings have to do with such things as the forgiveness of past sins, the right to pray and the like.

3. God has always put His spiritual blessings in something. Today's spiritual blessings are "in Christ" (Ephesians 1:3). In this study, we take a look at some of these spiritual blessings.

Discussion

I. A new creature:

   A. 2 Corinthians 5:17

   B. One is "the old man" before he is in Christ (Colossians 3:1-9).

   C. Read and study Romans 6:1-6.

II. The forgiveness of sins:

   A. Ephesians 1:7

   B. One does not have his past sins forgiven until he gets into Christ.

   C. Matthew 26:26-28; Romans 6:3-4

III. Redemption:

   A. Romans 3:24

- B. Jesus paid the price for our redemption when He shed His blood on the cross (1 Corinthians 6:20; Acts 20:28; 1 Peter 1:18-19).

IV. Peace:

- A. John 16:33
- B. Peace that "passeth all understanding" is in Christ (Philippians 4:6-7).

V. God's chosen people:

- A. Ephesians 1:4
- B. God has always had those known has His people. Today, they are Christians (Acts 11:26; 26:28; 1 Peter 4:16; 1 Peter 2:9-10).

VI. Salvation:

- A. 2 Timothy 2:10
- B. One cannot enjoy the blessing of salvation outside of Christ (Acts 4:12).

VII. Hope of eternal life:

- A. Eternal life is in the world to come (Mark 10:29-30).
- B. If one is in Christ, he has the hope and promise of eternal life (Ephesians 1:11; 1 John 5:11; 1 John 2:25; 1 Peter 1:3-4; Revelation 14:13).

Conclusion

Must get into Christ for these blessings (Galatians 3:27: Romans 6; 3-4)!

~ 14 ~
The Things of God
Matthew 22:21

Introduction

1. The Bible refers to "the things of God" (Matthew 22:21).
2. We would do well to learn of these things.

Discussion

I. The word of God:
   A. 1 John 2:14
   B. Shows the word is of God (Galatians 1:11-12)
   C. Psalm 119:89; 1 Thessalonians 2:13

II. The love of God:
   A. 1 John 2:5
   B. 1 John 4:9
   C. John 3:16; Romans 5:8; 1 John 5:3

III. The will of God:
   A. Hebrews 10:9-10
   B. 1 John 2:15-17; Matthew 7:21; Romans 10:1-3

IV. The church of God:
   A. 1 Corinthians 1:2
   B. 1 Timothy 3:15; Acts 20:28
   C. Whatever belongs to God belongs to Christ (John 16:15; John 17:10).

V. Born of God:
- A. The new birth (1 John 3:9; John 3:1-6)
- B. 1 Peter 1:22-23; James 1:18; 1 Corinthians 4:15

VI. The higher powers of God:
- A. Romans 13:1-7; 1 Peter 2:13-14
- B. Pray for these (1 Timothy 2:1-2).

VII. The children of God:
- A. 1 John 3:1-2, 10; 1 John 5:2; Galatians 3:26-27
- B. Are you a child of God?

Conclusion

1. Need to respect the things of God.
2. Have you obeyed God?

~ 15 ~
What It Means to Preach Christ
Acts 8:5

Introduction

1. It was apostolic practice to preach Christ (Acts 8:5).

2. This is the only kind of preaching which pleases God (1 Peter 1:25; 1 Corinthians 1:21). This was the kind of preaching that converted the eunuch (Acts 8:35-39).

3. So, we look at what it means to preach Christ:

Discussion

I. Preach the sonship of Jesus:

   A. Acts 9:20

   B. This was the claim of Jesus (John 1:1-2; Luke 1:26-35; Romans 1:4).

II. Preach the gospel of Christ:

   A. The commission for the apostles (Mark 16:15-16)

   B. 1 Corinthians 1:23; 15:1-2; Romans 1:16-17; Ephesians 1:13

III. Preach the kingdom of God:

   A. Acts 8:5; Acts 8:12

   B. To preach about the kingdom is to preach about the church (Matthew 16:18, 19; Hebrews 12:23, 28).

IV. Preach the name of Christ:

   A. Many think one name is as good as another. Not so!

   B. Philippians 2:9; Colossians 3:17

    C. The name indicates authority (Matthew 28:18; Matthew 7:29; John 2:5; John 7:46).

V. Preach beginning where the learner is:

    A. Philip began his preaching where the eunuch was in his understanding (Acts 8:35).

    B. Must do this today.

VI. Preach with an open book and mouth:

    A. Philip "opened his mouth" and the scriptures (Acts 8:35-39).

    B. Some hardly open their mouth or the Bible when they speak!

VII. Preach baptism:

    A. The reason those in Samaria were baptized was the preaching of Christ (Acts 8:5; Acts 8:12).

    B. Ever wonder why the eunuch wanted to be baptized (Acts 8:35-36)?

Conclusion

1. This is the only way to preach Christ.

2. Come and obey the Lord as we sing!

~ 16 ~
And Satan Came Also Among Them
Job 1:6

Introduction

1. Satan is our most dangerous enemy, as expressed in the parable of the tares (Matthew 13:24-30, 36-43).

2. We must never forget that our life is the target of the devil.

3. This lesson takes a look at when Satan came among some people.

Discussion

I. In the garden of Eden:

    A. God placed the first people, Adam and Eve, in the Eden garden, to "dress and keep it; not to eat of the tree of knowledge of good and evil." If they ate, they would surely die (Genesis 2:8-17).

    B. Satan came among them (Genesis 3:1-6) and lied to them. They ate, and sin entered into the world (Romans 5:12).

    C. The devil used his three avenues of temptation (1 John 2:15-17).

II. When God's people presented themselves before Him:

    A. Job 1:6; 2:1

    B. Job 2:3, 6

    C. Satan comes among the best of God's people!

    D. When we meet to worship, better watch out!

III. When Jesus had just been baptized:
   A. Matthew 3:13-17
   B. What better time to try to tempt Jesus? He had not eaten for a while (Matthew 4:1-11). Notice how Satan tempted Jesus.
   C. Jesus had hid the word in His heart (Psalm 119:11). He said: "It is written." He resisted Satan (James 4:7-8). We can too (1 Corinthians 10:13).

IV. When there were apostles:
   A. What better group to work among (Luke 22:1-6; John 13:1-2)?
   B. Judas betrayed our Lord (Matthew 26:14-25).
   C. Simon (Luke 22:31-34; Luke 22:54-62)

V. When some early Christians came into some money:
   A. Ananias and Sapphira (Acts 5:1-11)
   B. 1 Timothy 6:10-11

VI. When the sower sows the seed:
   A. Luke 8:5-15; Mark 4:1-20
   B. The devil knows that if he can steal the word out of the heart, there will be no obedience (Roman 10:17).

VII. Therefore:
   A. We must not be ignorant of Satan's devices (2 Corinthians 2:11).
   B. Satan will take advantage of us (2 Corinthians 2:11).
   C. He is a liar (John 8:44; 2 Thessalonians 2:9).
   D. Will hinder you (Galatians 5:7; 1 Thessalonians 2:18)
   E. Is a tempter (Matthew 4:1-3; 1 Corinthians 7:1-5)
   F. Is subtile (Genesis 3:1-2; 2 Corinthians 11:3)
   G. Can be transformed into an angel of light (2 Corinthians 11:14-15)
   H. Our adversary (1 Peter 5:8-9)
   I. A deceiver (Revelation 12:9)

J. God of this world (2 Corinthians 4:4)

K. Beelzebub (Matthew 12:24)

L. Dragon, serpent, devil, accuser (Revelation 12:9-10)

Conclusion

1. Be aware of this enemy.
2. Don't let him deceive you.

~ 17 ~
Who Am I?
Exodus 3:11

Introduction

1. Some people are facing an identity crisis, in that they don't really know who they are. Folks have been heard to say, "I'm going off to find myself!"
2. Moses asked: "Who am I" (Exodus 3:11)?
3. The Bible identifies who we really are. This lesson should be divided into two parts, perhaps one in the morning and one at the evening service.

Discussion

I. One made in the image of God:
   A. Genesis 1:26-27
   B. Genesis 2:7
   C. Zechariah 12:1; Job 32:8
   D. We are two men (2 Corinthians 4:16-18; 2 Corinthians 5:1-2).

II. The object of God's love:
   A. John 3:16
   B. Romans 5:8
   C. Everyone needs to know that they are loved by God!

III. One subject to God's laws:
   A. If not subject to God's laws, what makes man a sinner (1 John 3:4)?

    B. The word "whosoever" teaches us to be obedient.
        1. Acts 2:21
        2. Romans 10:13-16
        3. Revelation 22:17
    C. Ephesians 5:24

IV. A Christian:
    A. Acts 11:16; 26:28; 1 Peter 4:16
    B. We belong to Christ (1 Corinthians 6:19-20).

V. A child in God's family:
    A. A great song to sing: "God's Family" (1 Timothy 3:15)
    B. Born into it (Ephesians 3:15; John 3:3-5)

VI. A sheep in a flock:
    A. Acts 20:28
    B. Christ as the chief shepherd (John 10:1-16; 1 Peter 5:4)

VII. Soldiers in God's army:
    A. 2 Timothy 2:3-4
    B. With Christ as our captain (Hebrews 2:10)
    C. Armor to put on (Ephesians 6:10-18); fighting a spiritual war (2 Corinthians 10:4-5)

VIII. A branch on the vine:
    A. John 15:1-8
    B. Must bear fruit or be cut off
    C. Branches are not churches but individuals.

IX. A lively stone in a spiritual house:
    A. 1 Peter 2:5
    B. 1 Corinthians 3:11; Ephesians 2:20-22

X. A servant of righteousness:
    A. Romans 6:17-18
    B. Romans 6:3-4

    C. If you don't want to be a servant, just don't become a Christian!
XI. Strangers in a weary land:
    A. 1 Peter 1:17; 2:1
    B. Hebrews 11:13
    C. A good song to sing
XII. Member of the body of Christ:
    A. The church is the body of Christ (Colossians 1:24; Ephesians 1:22-23).
    B. The church is not one member but many (1 Corinthians 12:14). Note how one becomes a member (1 Corinthians 12:13).
XIII. A citizen in the kingdom of God:
    A. The church is the kingdom (Matthew 16:18-19; Hebrews 12:23, 28).
    B. Acts 17:7; Revelation 17:14; Colossians 1:13
XIV. Redeemed:
    A. Sing songs about being redeemed.
    B. Job 19:25; Titus 2:14; Ephesians 1:7; Romans 3:24

Conclusion

1. Now that you know who you are, be who you are supposed to be!
2. If not a child of God, come now obeying.

~ 18 ~
Sabbath Keeping
Deuteronomy 5:15

Introduction

1. Whether to keep the Sabbath day or the first day of the week is a question that only the Bible can settle.

2. So we make our appeal to the word of God as we ask, "For what saith the scripture" about Sabbath keeping (Romans 4:3)?

Discussion

I. Sabbath keeping belongs to the Jewish age:

   A. For the first 2,500 years, there was no command for or an example of anyone keeping the Sabbath day, except in Exodus 16:4 when God tested His people!

   B. For the next 1,500 years, during the law of Moses, we read of the command, "Remember the Sabbath day, to keep it holy" (Exodus 20:8). A man was stoned for violating Sabbath day regulations (Number 15:32-36)!

II. Beginning of Sabbath keeping:

   A. It did not begin in Genesis 1, as many teach.

   B. It began when Israel came out of the house of bondage (Exodus 20:2-2, 8). For the Sabbath day to be binding, one must have been a slave in Egypt!

   C. Nehemiah 9:13-14

III. Purpose of Sabbath keeping:

   A. A memorial to the Jews being delivered from Egyptian bondage (Deuteronomy 5:15)

B. A sign between God and Israel (Exodus 31:12-17; Ezekiel 20:10-12)

IV. Sabbath keepers fail to keep the Sabbath:

A. Those claiming to keep the Sabbath day do not follow the Lord's instructions. It was a day of rest (Exodus 35:1-3; 20:8-10). A lamb was offered on that day (Numbers 28:9-10). Travel was restricted (Exodus 16:29-30; Acts 1:12).

B. If binding, we must keep it as the Lord demanded!

V. Sabbath day done away:

A. This law was written on two tablets of stone (Exodus 34:28; Deuteronomy 4:13; 9:9-11). The law of Moses or the Law of God, being the same law (Ezra 7:6), has been done away (Galatians 4:21-31).

B. Jeremiah 31:31-34; Hebrews 8:7-13

C. Romans 7:1-6—now note Romans 7:7; Exodus 20:17

D. 2 Corinthians 3:6-14; Exodus 34:27-35

E. Colossians 2:14-16; Ephesians 2:15-16; Galatians 6:2

VI. The New Testament binds the first day of the week:

A. Mark 16:9; John 20:1, 19, 26

B. Acts 2 took place on the first day of the week (Leviticus 23:15-16). The New Testament Church began on the first day of the week (Acts 2:47)!

C. Acts 20:7; 1 Corinthians 16:1-2

Conclusion

1. The Sabbath day served its purpose, and God took it out of the way.

2. We must not bind where God has loosed!

~ 19 ~
Bible Works
John 6:29

Introduction

1. There is much misunderstanding about the works mentioned in the Bible.
2. Some think there is nothing one can do to be saved. A failure to know that some works save and some don't have led to this misunderstanding.

Discussion

I. Works of God:

   A. John 6:28-29

   B. Believing is not a work that God does, but He commands it (John 8:24; Hebrews 11:6; Mark 16:16).

II. Works of faith:

   A. 1 Thessalonians 1:3

   B. Faith must be expressed in obedience (James 2:14-26), like those in Hebrews 11!

III. Works of righteousness:

   A. Righteousness has to do with God's commandments (Acts 10:34-35; Psalm 119:172).

   B. Works that man might dream up do not save (Titus 3:5; Romans 10:1-3).

IV. Good works:

   A. Every Christian must be engaged in good works (Titus 3:1).

B. The Lord's church is never charged with good works, just individuals.
V. Works of the law of Moses:
   A. Galatians 2:16
   B. Some have falsely concluded because we are not justified by the works of the old law, there are no works to be done to be saved!
VI. Works of the flesh:
   A. Galatians 5:19-21
   B. Doing these works will cause one to be lost!
VII. Works of darkness:
   A. Romans 13:12
   B. Ephesians 5:11
VIII. Boastful works:
   A. Ephesians 2:8-10
   B. These kinds of works will not save!
   C. Notice verse 10: the word "workmanship!"
IX. Wicked works:
   A. Colossians 1:21
   B. Not saved by such
X. Dead works:
   A. Hebrews 6:1; 9:14
   B. James 2:26

Conclusion
1. Be sure to know the different kind of works.
2. Come and obey the works of God.

~ 20 ~
What Can Be Done With the Scriptures
2 Timothy 3:16-17

Introduction

1. The words "scripture" and "scriptures" can be found almost 50 times in the Bible. The word means "a writing."
2. There are a number of things that can be done with the scriptures.

Discussion

I. Read:
   A. Mark 12:10
   B. Acts 8:28, 32; 1 Timothy 4:13; Revelation 1:3

II. Believed:
   A. John 2:22
   B. Hebrews 11:6

III. Fulfilled:
   A. Luke 4:21
   B. Luke 24:44; Matthew 26:56

IV. Can be known:
   A. Matthew 22:29
   B. John 8:32; 2 Timothy 3:15

V. Searched:
   A. John 5:39
   B. Much needed today (Acts 17:11)

VI. Wrested:
    A. 2 Peter 3:16
    B. To twist
VII. Draws conclusion:
    A. Galatians 3:22
    B. Must reach scriptural conclusions

Conclusion

1. Read, study, and obey the Scriptures.
2. Come and do so just now!

~ 21 ~
These Are the Greatest
Luke 1:49

Introduction

1. The Bible describes a number of things as being great things.

2. This study takes a look at some of the great things of the Bible.

Discussion

I. The goodness of God:

  A. Psalm 31:19

  B. He can also be severe (Romans 11:22)!

II. The works of God:

  A. Psalm 92:5

  B. Exodus 14:31; Exodus 14:21-30

III. The sum of God's word:

  A. Psalm 139:17; Psalm 119:160

  B. It takes all that God says on a subject to have the sum.

IV. Salvation:

  A. Hebrews 2:3

  B. Salvation is divided into two parts: salvation from past sins at primary obedience (Acts 2:38) and salvation eternal at the end (Romans 13:11; 1 Peter 1:5, 9).

V. Gulf:

  A. Luke 16:26

      B. Relate the story (Luke 16:19-31).
VI. Reward:
      A. Matthew 5:12
      B. Matthew 16:27
      C. 1 Corinthians 3:8, 9

Conclusion

1. Obey the gospel and receive the great salvation.
2. Be faithful and reap the great reward!

~ 22 ~
Unto God Be the Glory
Ephesians 3:21

Introduction

1. A great way to begin this worship is to sing "To God Be The Glory."
2. To glorify God is to extol, praise and magnify Him as we ascribe honor to Him.
3. Exodus 40:34-35; Romans 3:23; 1 Corinthians 10:31
4. We examine some ways we glorify God.

Discussion

I. In the name Christian:
   A. 1 Peter 4:16
   B. Need to show "Christ living in us" (Galatians 2:20)

II. In fruit-bearing:
   A. John 15:1-8
   B. Proverbs 11:30; Galatians 5:22-23

III. In example-setting:
   A. Matthew 5:14-16
   B. Good works must be done by individual Christians (Philippians 2:15).
   C. 2 Corinthians 3:2

IV. In our body:
   A. 1 Corinthians 6:20

       B. We are not our own anymore (1 Corinthians 6:19).
V. In the church:
       A. Ephesians 3:21
       B. God is to have the glory, not the church.
       C. As a member of the Lord's church, we glorify God in our work, worship, teaching others and the like.
       D. There is no way one can glorify God outside the Lord's church!

Conclusion

1. Come, obey the gospel and begin to glorify God.
2. We stand waiting for your coming.

~ 23 ~
By the Blood of Christ
1 John 1:7

Introduction

1. The word "blood" is certainly a Bible study, in that it occurs 379 times in the Bible.
2. This biblical lesson takes a look at the phrase: "by the blood of Christ."

Discussion

I. We are made nigh:

    A. Ephesians 2:13

    B. Contrast the words "far off" and "nigh."

II. The New Testament came:

    A. Matthew 26:26-28

    B. This means that we live under the law of Christ (Galatians 6:2; Hebrews 9:15-18).

III. Propitiation made:

    A. 1 John 2:2; 1 John 4:10; Romans 3:25

    B. Such would not exist without His blood!

IV. We can be justified:

    A. Romans 5:6-10

    B. His blood can make us just in the sight of God!

    C. No wonder we can sing "Nothing but the Blood."

V. Redemption is available:
   A. Ephesians 1:7; Romans 3:24
   B. 1 Peter 1:18-19; Colossians 1:14
VI. There can be peace:
   A. Colossians 1:20
   B. John 16:33; Philippians 4:6-7
VII. Purge conscience:
   A. Hebrews 12:14
   B. Makes for a clean conscience
VIII. We can be washed from our sins:
   A. Revelation 1:5
   B. Hebrews 9:22; Hebrews 10:1-4

Conclusion

1. When you are baptized into the death of Christ, you can contact His blood and have your sins washed away (John 19:33-34; Romans 6:3-4; Acts 22:16).

2. Why not take care of this right now?

~ 24 ~
Before and After Baptism
Mark 16:15-16

Introduction

1. There is a time before and after baptism.
2. This study takes a look at what the Bible says before and after one is baptized.

Discussion

I. Before baptism:

   A. We are sinners.

      1. Sin separates man from God (Isaiah 59:1-2).

      2. "Sin is the transgression of the law" (1 John 3:4).

   B. We are "without Christ, aliens, strangers, having no hope, and without God in the world" (Ephesians 2:11-12).

   C. Have you ever wondered what all this means?

      1. Without Christ: it keeps one from all spiritual blessings (Ephesians 1:3).

      2. Aliens: it makes one a foreigner to the things of God.

      3. Strangers: one who does not have a covenant relationship with God.

      4. No hope: we are saved by hope (Romans 8:24), as hope anchors the soul (Hebrews 6:18-19).

      5. Without God: a person without God has no spiritual father (Ephesians 4:6).

      6. In the world: one in the world has the devil as his god (2 Corinthians 4:4).
II. After baptism:
    A. Past sins remitted (Acts 2:38); every sin washed away (Acts 22:16)
    B. Gift of the Holy Spirit (Acts 2:38-39): the promise of salvation
    C. Raised to walk in newness (Romans 6:3-34), being baptized into Christ (Galatians 3:27)
    D. Added to the church (Acts 2:47), as baptism puts one in the church (1 Corinthians 12:13)
    E. Now a Christian (Acts 11:26; Acts 26:28; 1 Peter 4:16)
    F. An observing servant (Matthew 28:19-20), involving being faithful (Revelation 2:10) and fruitful (Romans 6:22)
    G. Must continue (Colossians 1:23), being stedfast (1 Corinthians 15:58), holding fast to our profession of faith without wavering (Hebrews 12:23)
    H. Then exercise thyself...unto godliness (1 Timothy 4:7-8).

Conclusion

1. You are urged to be baptized today.
2. Enjoy the blessing after baptism.

~ 25 ~
A Good Soldier of Jesus Christ
2 Timothy 2:3-4

Introduction

1. The Bible identifies Christians as soldiers marching under the blood-stained banner of Christ (2 Timothy 2:3-4).
2. Jesus is the "captain of our salvation" (Hebrews 2:10).
3. We are calling attention to some characteristics of a good soldier.

Discussion

I. Endures hardness:

   A. 2 Timothy 2:3

   B. Hardness will come (2 Timothy 3:12).

   C. Salvation is promised to him that endures (Matthew 10:22).

II. Is not entangled:

   A. 2 Timothy 2:4

   B. The soldier has been called out of the world (1 Timothy 6:12; 1 Peter 2:9; and must not get bogged down with the affairs of life (Luke 8:14).

III. Is not afraid to fight:

   A. There is no room in the Lord's army for cowards (Judges 7:3).

   B. The Lord is looking for courageous soldiers who will fight with all their might (Ephesians 6:10; 1 Timothy 1:18).

IV. Is not ignorant of the enemy:

   A. 2 Corinthians 2:11

      B. Satan is subtle (2 Corinthians 11:3), deceives (Revelation 20:10), hinders (1 Thessalonians 2:18), and must be resisted (James 4:7).

V. Is well equipped:

      A. Ephesians 6:10-17

      B. A Christian is well equipped when he puts on the whole armor of God.

Conclusion

1. Enlist in the Lord's army today (by faith, repentance, confession and baptism).

2. Unsheathe the sword, fight to the end, and gain the victory! (1 Corinthians 15:57; 2 Timothy 4:6-8).

~ 26 ~
Great Things in the Book of Jonah
Jonah

Introduction

1. Sometimes the little Bible books are overlooked in our study.
2. The little book of Jonah has some great things in it. Let's notice some.

Discussion

I. Great call:

   A. Jonah 1:1-2

   B. Jonah was called to go preach to the people of Ninevah (Jonah 3:4)

   C. We are called by the gospel to go preach (2 Thessalonians 2:14; 2 Timothy 2:2).

II. Great city:

   A. Ninevah (Jonah 1:2; 1:2; 3:2-3; 4:11)

   B. Capital city of the great Assyrian empire

   C. Population estimated at 1,000,000

   D. A wicked city (Jonah 1:2)

III. Great flight:

   A. Jonah rose up to flee (Jonah 1:3) in the opposite direction.

   B. It is impossible to flee from the Lord's presence (Psalm 139:7-12)!

IV. Great wind and fish:

   A. The Lord sent a great wind (Jonah 1:4).

   B. He also sent a great fish to swallow up Jonah (Jonah 1:17). The New Testament calls it a whale (Matthew 12:40).

V. Great repentance:

   A. Ninevah repented (Jonah 3:4-9; Matthew 12:41).

   B. God spared the city (Jonah 3:10).

   C. We must also repent (Acts 17:30).

VI. Great kindness:

   A. God is of great kindness (Jonah 4:2).

   B. God was very kind in saving these people, and His kindness today is shown toward us through Christ (Ephesians 2:7).

Conclusion

1. Some great things for our learning (Romans 15:4)

2. Salvation is of the Lord!

~ 27 ~
Some Who Cannot Please God
1 Corinthians 10:5

Introduction

1. Our chief desire must be to please God (Colossians 1:10; 1 Thessalonians 4:1; 1 John 3:22).

2. The Bible records some who pleased God and those with whom God was not pleased (Hebrews 11:4; 1 Corinthians 10:5).

3. Let's look at some who cannot please God.

Discussion

I. Folks without faith:

   A. Hebrews 11:6

   B. John 8:24

   C. Faith comes by hearing the word (Romans 10:17).

II. They that are in the flesh:

   A. Romans 8:8

   B. There are two groups of people: the fleshly and the spiritual (Romans 8:1-14).

   C. Discuss Galatians 5:16-25.

III. Children who disobey their parents:

   A. Colossians 3:20

   B. Ephesians 6:1-2

   C. The Law of Moses taught respect for parental authority (Exodus 20:12; Leviticus 19:3; Deuteronomy 21:18-21).

IV. Individuals who please themselves:
   A. Romans 15:1, 3
   B. You cannot just do what pleases you and at the same time be pleasing to God!
V. Those who try to please men:
   A. Galatians 1:10
   B. You may please men but not be pleasing to God.
   C. Saul, an example (1 Samuel 15:24)
VI. Entangled soldiers:
   A. 2 Timothy 2:4
   B. The cares of this life choke the word (Luke 8:14).
   C. This gets in the way of many today and keeps them from pleasing God.

Conclusion

1. Is God pleased with you this day?
2. Be an Enoch (Genesis 5:24; Hebrews 11:5).
3. Won't you come and do those things that please God?

~ 28 ~
What We Must Do With Truth
John 8:32

Introduction

1. There is nothing more important than truth (John 18:38; John 17:17).
2. Here are some things we must do with truth.

Discussion

I. Buy it:

    A. Proverbs 23:23; Matthew 13:44

    B. Buy it at any cost and hold on to it!

II. Know it:

    A. John 8:32; 1 Timothy 2:3-4

    B. To know the truth, we must read and study (Ephesians 3:4; 2 Timothy 2:15).

III. Rightly divide it:

    A. 2 Timothy 2:15

    B. Some divide the truth wrongly to their destruction (2 Peter 3:16).

IV. Believe it:

    A. 2 Thessalonians 2:12

    B. Mark 16:16; John 20:30-31

V. Love it:

    A. 2 Thessalonians 2:10-12

　　　　B. Like the Psalmist (Psalms 119:97; 113, 127, 140, 165, 167)

VI. Obey it:

　　　　A. 1 Peter 1:22

　　　　B. Will do no good to buy it, know it, rightly divide it, believe it and love it unless we obey it!

VII. Speak it:

　　　　A. Proverbs 12:17

　　　　B. Ephesians 4:15, 25

VIII. Walk in it:

　　　　A. Galatians 2:11-14

　　　　B. 2 John 4, 6; 3 John 3-4

Conclusion

1. You have heard the truth. Now you know it. Do you believe it and love it enough to obey and walk in it?

2. This is the favorite time and place to obey the truth. Come now!

~ 29 ~
What We Must Not Do With Truth
Proverbs 23:23

Introduction

1. As there are some things we must do with truth, there are some things we must not do with it.
2. Let's notice a few.

Discussion

I. Sell it:

   A. Proverbs 23:23

   B. Some will sell the truth for a little bit of nothing!

II. Change it:

   A. Romans 1:25

   B. There are warnings against changing the truth (Deuteronomy 4:2; 12:32; Proverbs 30:6; 1 Corinthians 4:6; 2 John 9; Revelation 22:18-19).

III. Turn our ears away from it:

   A. 2 Timothy 4:4

   B. Like those of old, many today cry, "speak unto us smooth things" (Isaiah 30:10).

   C. Faithful preachers preach it when we want to hear it and when we don't (2 Timothy 4:2).

IV. Resist it:

   A. 2 Timothy 3:8

B. As Jannes and Jambres withstood Moses (Exodus 7:10-13), some today fight against the truth.

V. Lie against it:

   A. James 3:14

   B. All lies are against the truth (1 John 2:21).

   C. Turn away from truth-resisters (2 Timothy 3:5).

VI. Take it out of our mouths:

   A. Psalm 119:43

   B. Proverbs 8:7

   C. We must always be found speaking the truth (Ephesians 4:15, 25).

VII. Err from it:

   A. 2 Timothy 2:18

   B. Fables and commandments of men who turn from the truth (Titus 1:14).

Conclusion

What have you been doing with truth?

~ 30 ~
Precious Things in the Epistles of Peter
1 Peter 2:4-7

Introduction

1. In the Bible, lots of things are said to be precious.

2. Let's notice some precious things from the writings of Peter.

Discussion

I. Precious trial of faith:

   A. 1 Peter 1:7

   B. Peter compares the trial of one's faith with the trial of gold.

II. Precious blood of Christ:

   A. 1 Peter 1:18-19

   B. The blood of Christ is precious because of what it does:

      1. Justifies (Romans 5:9)

      2. Redeems (Ephesians 1:7)

      3. Cleanses (1 John 1:7)

      4. Washes (Revelation 1:5)

      5. Remits sins (Matthew 26:28)

      6. Sanctifies (Hebrews 13:12)

III. Precious Christ:

   A. 1 Peter 2:4, 7

   B. Christ is not precious to all, only to those who believe (1 Peter 2:8).

    C. Christ is precious because of His life, death, and resurrection.

IV. Precious faith:

    A. 2 Peter 1:1

    B. The precious faith is obtained from hearing the word of God (Romans 10:17).

    C. Note what can happen to one's faith (1 Timothy 1:19; 2 Timothy 2:17-18).

V. Precious promises:

    A. 2 Peter 1:4

    B. Observe some of the precious promises of the Bible:

        1. Promises to Abraham (Genesis 12)

        2. Promise of salvation to those who believe and are baptized (Mark 16:16)

        3. Promise to hear our prayers (1 John 5:14; 1 Peter 3:12)

Conclusion

Are these things precious to you?

~ 31 ~
The Great Commission
Matthew 28:18-20

Introduction

1. The Great Commission is found in Matthew 28:18-20; Mark 16:15-16; Luke 24:46-47.
2. Here are some great things about the Great Commission.

Discussion

I. One with great authority:
   A. Matthew 28:18 (Christ)
   B. Matthew 7:29
   C. John 2:5; 7:46
   D. This authority was given to Christ by the Father (Ephesians 1:21-23).

II. A great charge:
   A. There is no greater charge than to "go teach" or "preach" (Matthew 28:19; Mark 16:15).
   B. This is the only way men have of knowing God's will (John 6:44-45).

III. A great group of people:
   A. All nations (Matthew 28:19; Luke 24:47)
   B. The gospel is for all.

IV. A great message:
   A. Mark 16:15

      B. Luke 24:47

      C. The gospel message of repentance and remission of sins is the greatest message!

V. A great plan of salvation:

      A. Mark 16:16

      B. Belief + Baptism = Salvation

VI. A great promise:

      A. Matthew 28:20

      B. There is no greater promise than the Lord's promise to be with His people!

VII. A great beginning:

      A. Luke 24:47

      B. The Great Commission was executed for the first time on the day of Pentecost (Acts 2).

Conclusion

1. May we have greater appreciation for the Great Commission.

2. Have you heard, believed, and obeyed?

~ 32 ~
Happy Is the Man
Proverbs 3:13

Introduction

1. The people of God have always been a happy people (Deuteronomy 33:29; Psalm 144:15).
2. We make use of the phrase: "Happy is the man" to describe the happy man.

Discussion

I. Whom God correcteth:

   A. Job 5:17
   B. Proverbs 3:11-12
   C. Hebrews 12:5-11
   D. The Scriptures are designed to make us happy: "for correction" (2 Timothy 3:16-17).

II. That hath his quiver full:

   A. Psalm 17:3-5
   B. Children can add an element of happiness to the home.

III. That feareth the Lord:

   A. Psalm 128
   B. Psalm 112:1
   C. Discuss what it means to fear the Lord; it includes respect for God.

IV. That hath God for his help:

- A. Psalm 146:5
- B. God has always been a help to those who put their hope in Him. Notice some examples:
  1. Moses (Exodus 18:4)
  2. Asa (2 Chronicles 14:11-13)

V. That findeth wisdom:
- A. Proverbs 3:13-26
- B. Wisdom is found in keeping God's commandments (Deuteronomy 4:5-6).

VI. That condemneth not himself:
- A. Romans 14:22
- B. The context concerns authorized liberties, where every person is to be fully persuaded in his own mind (Romans 14:5).

VII. Who endures:
- A. James 5:11
- B. First Peter teaches endurance (1 Peter 2:19-20; 3:14; 4:12-16).

Conclusion

How do you measure up with the happy man?

~ 33 ~
The Holy Scriptures
2 Timothy 3:16-17

Introduction

1. Let's take a careful look at 2 Timothy 3:15-17.
2. We will notice some things about the holy Scriptures.

Discussion

I. May be known:

   A. Timothy knew them from his youth (2 Timothy 3:15).

   B. The Scriptures may be known through the teaching of others and personal study (2 Timothy 2:2; 2 Timothy 2:15).

   C. Jesus taught: "Search the scriptures" (John 5:39).

II. Are able to make men wise:

   A. 2 Timothy 3:15

   B. Only the holy Scriptures are able to do this.

III. Are given by inspiration of God:

   A. 2 Timothy 3:16

   B. The phrase "inspiration of God" means God-breathed truths into the writers and is of God.

   C. 2 Peter 1:21

IV. Are profitable:

   A. The holy Scriptures are profitable for: doctrine, reproof, correction in righteousness (2 Timothy 3:16).

   B. May we use the Scriptures for that which God intended!

V. Makes the man of God perfect:
   A. 2 Timothy 3:16-17
   B. "Perfect" means the man of God is made complete, as he uses the Scriptures for his profit.
   C. A failure to read, study, and apply the Scriptures will leave one imperfect!

VI. Thoroughly furnishes us unto all good works:
   A. 2 Timothy 3:17
   B. The Scriptures are sufficient in that they equip the man of God, so that he needs nothing else!
   C. Like Dorcas, we must be "full of good works" (Acts 9:36).
   D. Letting our light shine in good works is the duty of every child of God (Matthew 5:16).

Conclusion

1. Read, believe, and obey the Scriptures.
2. Ask: "For what saith the scripture" (Romans 4:3; Galatians 4:30).

~ 34 ~
Some Things to Be Found in Christians
2 Peter 1:5-11

Introduction

1. There are some things found in Christ.
2. As we get into Christ, there are some things that should be found in us.

Discussion

I. Christ:
   A. If we are in Christ, then Christ should be in us.
   B. John 15:4-5
   C. Galatians 2:20
   D. 2 Corinthians 5:15; 13:5

II. The mind of Christ:
   A. Philippians 2:5-8
   B. Discuss the mind Christ had.
   C. Is this mind in you?

III. The love of God:
   A. John 17:26
   B. 1 John 2:15
   C. 1 John 3:16-17
   D. 1 John 4:7-12

IV. The things of 2 Peter 1:5-7:

      A. Discuss each of these to be added to faith.

      B. Read 2 Peter 1:8-11

V. A readiness to preach the gospel:

      A. Romans 1:15

      B. Notice the readiness of Paul.

      C. This readiness is observed in early disciples as seen in Acts 8:4.

VI. Joy:

      A. John 15:11

      B. Philippians is the book of joy.

      C. Note the things that should fill us with joy.

VII. Hope:

      A. 1 Peter 3:15

      B. Hope saves (Romans 8:24) and anchors us (Hebrews 6:18-19).

Conclusion

1. Can these things be found in you?
2. Sometimes there are things found in us that ought not be found in Christians (Ephesians 4:25-31; Colossians 3:8-9; 1 Peter 2:1).

~ 35 ~
Praying Positions
1 Thessalonians 5:17

Introduction

1. Some teach that the only scriptural body position is kneeling while praying.
2. Others teach that one must bow the head.
3. The Bible offers a number of different body positions when praying.

Discussion

I. Standing:

   A. Luke 18:11

   B. This man stood and prayed.

II. Looking down:

   A. Luke 18:13

   B. This passage infers that one may look down and pray.

III. Looking up:

   A. John 17:1

   B. Jesus prayed as He looked up.

IV. Lifted up hands:

   A. 1 Timothy 2:8

   B. Paul alluded to the ancient practice of the "lifting up of hands" in petition to God in prayer.

V. Lying down:

      A. Matthew 26:39

      B. Jesus prayed in the garden lying prostrate on the ground.

VI. Kneeling:

      A. Acts 20:36

      B. We can read a number of times when men kneeled down when they prayed.

Conclusion

1. Since we have studied a number of different body positions, which one of these is now binding on Christians?

2. We must be careful not to bind where the Lord has not bound nor loose where He has bound!

~ 36 ~
The Music Passages
Hebrews 2:12

Introduction

1. God has specified the kind of music He wants in New Testament worship. When God specifies, all others are excluded.

2. We are looking at ten music passages in our study at this time.

Discussion

I. Matthew 26:30:

    A. Read the passage.

    B. Ask: What kind of music is this? Vocal or mechanical/instrumental?

II. Mark 14:26:

    A. How does this passage read?

    B. Vocal or mechanical/instrumental?

III. Acts 16:25:

    A. Paul and Silas were singing and praying.

    B. Note the kind of music.

IV. Romans 15:9:

    A. This is a quote from 2 Samuel 22:50; Psalm 18:49.

    B. What kind of music is this?

V. 1 Corinthians 14:15:

    A. The only passage that says we are to sing with something

B. What is it?

VI. Ephesians 5:19:

A. The instrument is the heart.

B. Whatever I am told to do here, you are also told to do. If mechanical/instrumental music is involved, each one would have to play. If not, why not?

VII. Colossians 3:16:

A. Singing teaches and admonishes.

B. Can a mechanical instrument do this?

VIII. Hebrews 2:12:

A. Note what kind of music is to be used in the church.

B. Was it playing or singing?

IX. Hebrews 13:15:

A. Singing comes as the fruit of our lips.

B. We need to just sing.

X. James 5:13:

A. Sing or play?

B. Vocal music is the command.

~ 37 ~
Living Below in This Old Sinful World
Romans 12:1-2

Introduction

1. The song "Where Could I Go" sets forth our need for the Lord as we live below in this old sinful world (it would be good to sing the song).
2. The Bible teaches us about living in this world.

Discussion

I. Live by the word of God:

   A. Matthew 4:4

   B. The word of God is as necessary to living as our daily bread.

II. Live by faith:

   A. Habakkuk 2:4; Romans 1:17

   B. Galatians 3:11; Hebrews 10:38

   C. Hebrews 11 records some who lived by faith in this old sinful world. Note some.

III. Live peaceably:

   A. Romans 12:18

   B. "Blessed are the peacemakers" (Matthew 5:9).

   C. "Live in peace" (2 Corinthians 13:11).

IV. Live for Jesus:

   A. 2 Corinthians 5:14-15

   B. We are not to live for ourselves or other men, but we are to live for Him who gave Himself for us! A good song about this could be "Live for Jesus."

V. Live soberly, righteously and godly:

    A. Titus 2:11-14

    B. The Scriptures often talk about honest living (Romans 13:13; 1 Thessalonians 4:12; 2 Corinthians 8:21; 1 Timothy 2:2; 1 Peter 2:12).

VI. Live unto righteousness:

    A. 1 Peter 2:24

    B. Romans 6 teaches us about living unto righteousness.

Conclusion

1. Where could I go but to the Lord?
2. Do you need to make some changes in your living? If so, come just now.

~ 38 ~
They That Were Ready
Matthew 25:10

Introduction

1. Read Matthew 25:1-13.

2. The Scriptures place emphasis on being ready.

Discussion

I. Ready to hear:

   A. Ecclesiastes 5:1-2

   B. James 1:19

   C. Ready to hear Christ (Matthew 17:5). He has the words of life (John 6:63, 68).

   D. Ready to hear the word (Acts 13:7). Faith comes this way (Romans 10:17).

II. Ready to preach the Gospel:

   A. Romans 1:15

   B. The gospel needs to be preached to every creature (Mark 16:15).

   C. The gospel saves (Romans 1:16; Ephesians 1:13), but it must be preached, believed and obeyed.

III. Ready for every good work:

   A. Titus 3:1

   B. 2 Timothy 2:21

   C. The Scriptures furnish us unto every good work

(2 Timothy 3:16-17).

   D. Good works belong to the individual Christian (Matthew 5:16).

IV. Ready to give answer:

   A. 1 Peter 3:15

   B. Colossians 4:6

   C. This emphasizes the importance of Bible study (2 Timothy 2:15).

V. Ready to distribute:

   A. 1 Timothy 6:18

   B. Romans 12:13

   C. We need to be liberal in our distribution among needy saints (2 Corinthians 9:13).

VI. Ready to die:

   A. Psalm 88:15

   B. Acts 21:13

   C. Death will come, ready or not (Ecclesiastes 9:5; 1 Corinthians 15:22; Hebrews 9:27. We must be ready!

Conclusion

"They that were ready went in with him" (Matthew 25:10). Those not ready faced a shut door! Are you ready? Come and obey, if not.

~ 39 ~
God's Law Concerning Marriage, Divorce and Remarriage
Matthew 19:3-9

Introduction

1. Many today marry, divorce, and remarry without considering God's law.

2. God's law is simple and is clearly revealed within His word, the Bible.

Discussion

I. God's law concerning marriage:

   A. God's law from the beginning involves one man for one woman for life.

   B. Genesis 2:18-24

   C. Matthew 19:3-9

   D. Romans 7:2-3

II. God's law concerning divorce:

   A. Today, men and women divorce for just about any reason imaginable, and our states allow no-fault divorce.

   B. Malachi 2:16

   C. There is only one Scriptural reason for divorce.

      1. Matthew 19:9; Matthew 5:32

      2. The Lord allows the party innocent of fornication to put away their fornicating mate.

D. To get a divorce for just any reason other than fornication is to get an unscriptural divorce. If you know of any other reason for divorce, where is the passage of Scripture allowing such?

III. God's law concerning remarriage:

   A. The Scriptures only show two groups of people who have the right to take another mate.

      1. Those whose mate is dead (Romans 7:2-3)

      2. Those who put away a mate for fornication (Matthew 19:9)

   B. For anyone else to marry another mate is to live in adultery. One can live in such a sin (Colossians 3:5-7).

   C. If you know of anyone else who has the right to take another mate, where is the Scripture?

Conclusion

1. Since marriage is of God (Genesis 2:18-24), let's learn to respect God's law governing this divine institution.

2. Parents need to begin teaching their children these truths early on!

~ 40 ~
Bible Examples of Bountiful Giving
John 3:16

Introduction

1. The Scriptures appeal to us to be bountiful givers (Romans 12:8; 2 Corinthians 9:6-7).

2. Bountiful giving is marked by abundance as it involves free and generous giving.

3. Let's notice some examples.

Discussion

I. Israel's giving for the tabernacle:

   A. Exodus 25:1-2

   B. Exodus 35:4-5, 20-22

   C. The people brought "much more than enough" (Exodus 36:1-7).

II. Israel's giving at temple dedication:

   A. 1 Kings 8:1-5, 62-66

   B. They sacrificed "sheep and oxen, that could not be told nor numbered for multitude" (1 Kings 8:1-5). The brazen altar "was too little to receive the burnt offerings" (1 Kings 8:62-66).

III. Israel's giving for house repairs:

   A. 2 Chronicles 24:4-14

   B. The Lord's house had been broken up and needed fixing up (2 Chronicles 24:7).

      C. They made a chest, set it without the gate and gathered money in abundance (2 Chronicles 24:8-11).

IV. Macedonians' giving for needy saints:

      A. 2 Corinthians 8:1-8

      B. They were in a state of poverty but gave liberally (2 Corinthians 8:2).

      C. They went beyond their power to help (2 Corinthians 8:3).

V. God's giving:

      A. Last but not least (James 1:17).

      B. Some things God has given:

          1. His grace (Titus 2:11)

          2. A book (2 Timothy 3:16-17)

          3. Life (1 John 5:11)

          4. His Son (John 3:16)

      C. No man can outgive God (Luke 6:38; Malachi 3:8-10).

Conclusion

These Biblical examples of bountiful giving should stir and stimulate us to evaluate our giving.

~ 41 ~
Kinds of Worship
John 4:24

Introduction

1. There are five different kinds of worship mentioned in the Bible. Of these, only one is acceptable to God.
2. Let's take a look, so our worship may be found pleasing unto God.

Discussion

I. Vain worship:

    A. Matthew 15:9

    B. That which is vain has no real value; it's for nought.

    C. When our heart is removed from our worship or we teach precepts of men, our worship becomes vain.

II. Mock worship:

    A. Mark 15:19-20

    B. This is worship that was insincere, in defiance, and in derision of Christ.

III. Ignorant worship:

    A. Acts 17:23

    B. The Athenians worshipped God but did so ignorantly.

    C. And so do many today!

IV. Will worship:

    A. Colossians 3:23

      B. To worship as we desire, without regard and respect for the will of the Lord, is to be guilty of will worship.

V. True worship:

      A. John 4:24

      B. True worship is directed to God in spirit (from the heart) and in truth (according to the word of God—John 17:17).

      C. This is the only kind of worship that is acceptable to God.

      D. This is the kind of worship New Testament Christians did (Acts 2:42; Hebrews 2:12; Ephesians 5:19).

Conclusion

1. Which kind of worship have you been offering to God?

2. "Give unto the Lord the glory due unto his name; worship the Lord in the beauty of holiness" (Psalm 29:2).

~ 42 ~
Saved Like Noah
Hebrews 11:7

Introduction

1. Our text for today's lesson is 1 Peter 3:20-21.
2. Noah's salvation is a type of our salvation.
3. This lesson compares the two salvations.

Discussion

I. Noah was saved by the grace of God:

　A. Genesis 6:8

　B. He was not saved by grace alone.

　C. We are saved by the grace of God (Ephesians 2:8, Titus 2:11).

II. Noah was saved by faith:

　A. Noah was not saved by faith alone (Hebrews 11:7).

　B. We are saved by faith (Hebrews 11:6; John 8:24; Romans 5:1).

　C. We are not saved by faith only (James 2:24).

III. Noah was saved by obedience:

　A. Genesis 6:22; 7:5

　B. Hebrews 11:7

　C. We are saved by obedience (Matthew 7:21; Luke 6:46; Hebrews 5:9).

IV. Noah was saved by water:

　A. 1 Peter 3:20

- B. Water buoyed up the ark and kept it afloat (Genesis 7:17).
- C. We are not saved by water; we are saved by baptism which means an immersion or burial in water (1 Peter 3:21; Mark 16:16; Acts 2:38; 22:16; 1 Peter 3:21; Acts 10:47-48; Acts 8:36-39).
- D. Baptism is a burial and a planting (Romans 6:3-3-5; Colossians 2:12).
- E. Baptism puts us into Christ (Galatians 3:27) and the church (1 Corinthians 12:13).

V. Noah was saved in the ark:
- A. Salvation from drowning was placed in the ark (Genesis 7:1, 7, 9, 13, 15-16, 23, 1 Peter 3:20).
- B. Today, salvation is in Christ (2 Timothy 2:10), and the saved are in the church (Acts 2:47; Ephesians 5:23).
- C. Baptism puts one into Christ (Galatians 3:27) and the church (1 Corinthians 12:13).
- D. Just as those outside the ark perished, all outside the Lord's church and Christ will be forever lost (Matthew 15:13)!

Conclusion

Noah was saved by grace, faith, obedience, water, and in the ark. Obey the Lord!

~ 43 ~
The One Body
Colossians 1:18

Introduction

1. Text to read: Ephesians 4:4
2. This sermon calls our attention to some basic things the Bible teaches about the one body.

Discussion

I. The body is the church:

    A. The church is the body (Ephesians 1:22-23), and the body is the church (Colossians 1:24). Thus, they are one and the same.

    B. Since there is but one body (1 Corinthians 12:20), and the body is the church, there is just one true church!

II. The body is headed by Christ:

    A. Ephesians 1:22-23

    B. Colossians 1:18

    C. Thus, the church is subject unto Christ in all things (Ephesians 5:23-24).

III. The body is where men are reconciled unto God:

    A. Ephesians 2:16

    B. Sin separates and alienates us from God.

        1. Isaiah 59:1-2

        2. Colossians 1:21

      C. The making of peace with God is possible in the one body (Colossians 1:20-22).

IV. The body contains the saved:

      A. Ephesians 5:23

      B. Acts 2:47

V. The body is to be free from division:

      A. 1 Corinthians 12:25

      B. One of the great pleas of the Bible is the plea for unity.

          1. John 17:20-21

          2. 1 Corinthians 1:10

          3. Psalm 133:1

VI. The body is entered by baptism:

      A. 1 Corinthians 12:13

      B. As one is baptized into Christ (Galatians 3:27), he enters the body of Christ as the Lord adds him to the church (Acts 2:41, 47).

Conclusion

1. Are you a member of the one body?

2. You are invited to be baptized into the one body (1 Corinthians 12:13).

~ 44 ~
When a Father Offered His Son
Hebrews 11:17-19

Introduction

1. Abraham offered up his only son, Isaac (Genesis 22:1-19; Hebrews 11:17-19).

2. Notice some valuable lessons from when a father offered his son.

Discussion

I. Our faith may be tested:

   A. In Genesis 22:1, the word "tempt" means God "tried" Abraham (Hebrews 11:17).

   B. This was a test to Abraham's faith.

   C. Would you have passed the test as Abraham did (Hebrews 11:17; Genesis 22:12)? Trial of our faith is called precious (1 Peter 1:7).

II. We must love God above all:

   A. Abraham loved his son (Genesis 22:2).

   B. Abraham did not offer his son because he did not love him, but because he loved God more!

   C. We must love God above everyone and everything (Matthew 10:37; 22:37).

III. We must be zealous in worship:

   A. Genesis 22:3-5

   B. Abraham's zeal is seen in that he rose up early to worship God! Some are always late for worship!

- C. We need this kind of zeal today (John 4:24; Titus 2:14).
- D. Not all that one does is worship. Abraham was said to "go yonder and worship" (Genesis 22:5). If everything Abraham did was worship, he would not have had to "go yonder and worship!" Right?

IV. Faith must be coupled with works:
- A. Hebrews 11:17-19
- B. James 2:21-24
- C. The faith that saves is the faith that obeys!

V. God provides for our needs:
- A. Genesis 22:7-8, 13-14
- B. Psalm 23
- C. Matthew 6:31-33

VI. God blesses the obedient:
- A. Genesis 22:15-18
- B. You can be blessed with faithful Abraham (Galatians 3:9; Ephesians 1:3).

Conclusion

The story of Abraham offering Isaac looked forward to God, the Father, sacrificing His Son for our sins (John 19:16-18). Come to Jesus today in obedience!

~ 45 ~
Respect for the Word of God
Nehemiah 8:7

Introduction

1. Nehemiah 8 is one of the finest places respect for the word of God is seen.

2. Observe the respect shown.

Discussion

I. They asked for it:

   A. Nehemiah 8:1

   B. What book do you ask for?

   C. May we always insist the men of God bring the book of God!

II. They listened to it:

   A. "From morning until midday" (Nehemiah 8:3)! Some can hardly sit a few minutes today.

   B. May we never grow tired of hearing the word of God!

III. They made provisions for it:

   A. Nehemiah 8:4

   B. Would you have made the arrangements these folks made?

IV. They stood up for it:

   A. Nehemiah 8:5

   B. Folks stand at the singing of the National Anthem or "Here Comes the Bride." Should we show any less respect for the word of God?

V. They were in agreement with it:
   A. Nehemiah 8:6
   B. "Amen" means I agree.

VI. They stood in their place:
   A. Nehemiah 8:7
   B. Let's learn to get in, stay in, and be satisfied in our place today.

VII. They wept over it:
   A. Nehemiah 8:9
   B. Ever shed a tear as the word of God is read?

VIII. They obeyed it:
   A. Nehemiah 8:13-18
   B. Would do us no good to ask for and listen to God's word, if we do not obey it!

Conclusion

We need the same respect for the word of God today! Come and obey it just now.

~ 46 ~
Men Needed in the Church
1 Corinthians 16:13

Introduction

1. The Lord's church is in need of some good men (Proverbs 2:20).
2. This study takes a look at some men needed in the church.

Discussion

I. Men who are righteous before God:
   A. Like Noah (Genesis 7:1; 2 Peter 2:5)
   B. A righteous man does righteousness (1 John 3:7).
   C. Eternal life is in store for the righteous (Matthew 25:46).

II. Men who command their household:
   A. Men like Abraham (Genesis 18:19)
   B. Ephesians 6:4
   C. A must for an elder in the church (1 Timothy 3:4-5, 12).

III. Men who are uncompromising:
   A. Like Moses (Exodus 10:24-26)
   B. We cannot afford to compromise with error (Galatians 2:4-5)!

IV. Men who choose to serve the Lord:
   A. Men like Joshua (Joshua 24:15)
   B. The church could stand some good men like this today!

V. Men who are mighty in the scriptures:

A. Like Apollos (Acts 18:24, 28).
B. Too many men do not know the Scripture as they should!
C. The only way one will become spiritually strong is by searching the Scriptures (John 5:39; Acts 17:11).

Conclusion

The church needs men to step us and be men! Are you one of them?

~ 47 ~
What Happens When You're Baptized
Mark 16:15-16

Introduction

1. The scriptures teach the necessity of baptism.
2. These seeds make us aware of some things which happen when you're baptized:

Discussion

I. You're saved:

    A. From your past sins, that is.

    B. Mark 16:16; 1 Peter 3:21

II. You're born again:

    A. John 3:3-5

    B. 1 Peter 1:23; James 1:18; 1 Corinthians 4:15

III. Your past sins are remitted:

    A. Acts 2:38

    B. Romans 3:25

    C. "Remission of sins" is forgiveness or pardon of sins.

IV. You receive the gift of the Holy Spirit:

    A. Acts 2:38

    B. This is the promise of salvation (Acts 2:39) as prophesied and revealed by the Holy Spirit (Joel 2:32; Acts 2:21).

V. You're added to the church:
   A. Acts 2:47
   B. 1 Corinthians 12:13
   C. Now you are ready to work in the Lord's vineyard (1 Corinthians 15:58); ready to worship God (John 4:24).

VI. Your sins are washed away:
   A. Acts 22:16
   B. Titus 3:5

VII. You reach the death of Christ and thereby contact the blood of Christ:
   A. Romans 6:3-4
   B. John 19:33-34

VIII. You're made free from sin:
   A. Notice the word "then" (Romans 6:17-18).
   B. The form of doctrine has been obeyed (Romans 6:3-4).

Conclusion

1. Have you been baptized?
2. If not, come just now.

~ 48 ~
Things Men Sold
Matthew 13:45-46

Introduction

1. The Bible uses commercial terms of buying and selling. The word "sold" can be found as many as 75 times in the Bible.

2. This Bible lesson takes a look to see some things the Bible says men sold.

Discussion

I. Esau sold his birthright:

   A. Genesis 25:33

   B. Hebrews 12:16

II. Joseph was sold:

   A. Genesis 37

   B. Psalm 105:17

   C. Acts 7:9

III. Israel was sold to their enemies:

   A. Judges 2

   B. Judges 2:14; 3:8; 4:2; 10:7 shows the people into whose hands God sold them.

   C. 1 Samuel 12:9; Lamentations 5:4

IV. Some sold themselves to work evil:

   A. Ahab (1 Kings 21:20)

   B. 1 Kings 21:25-26

       C. Isaiah 52:3; Proverbs 2:14
V. Some bought and sold doves in the temple:
       A. Matthew 21:12-13
       B. John 2:14-17
       C. Make some applications for today.
VI. Many sold under sin:
       A. Romans 7:14
       B. Romans 6:23; James 1:14-15
VII. Christians sold possessions:
       A. Acts 2:45; 4:34; 4:37
       B. Notice Acts 5:1-11 as a bad example.
VIII. Jesus sold for 30 pieces of silver:
       A. Matthew 26:15; 27:3-4
       B. Matthew 26:14-16; Matthew 27:3-10
IX. A merchant sold all he had:
       A. Matthew 13:45-46
       B. This transaction shows the great value of the gospel and the church!
       C. Romans 1:16-17; James 1:21; Acts 20:28; Acts 2:47

Conclusion

1. Review. Now "buy the truth and sell it not" (Proverbs 23:23)!
2. Need to obey the truth? Now is the right time and place (2 Corinthians 6:2).

~ 49 ~
Old Testament Hospitality
Hebrews 13:2

Introduction

1. Both the Old and New Testaments teach that the Lord's people must be hospitable.
2. Hospitality means a "lover of strangers."
3. This study is designed to inspire us to be "given to hospitality" (Romans 12:13).

Discussion

I. Abraham and Sarah:
   A. Genesis 18:1-8
   B. Would you have extended this hospitality, and do you have a wife like Sarah?

II. Lot:
   A. Genesis 19:1-9
   B. Very few today insist on folks accepting their hospitality!

III. Rebekah's family:
   A. Genesis 24 is a story of hospitality.
   B. Notice some phrases which show hospitality was offered.
   C. We need more families like this.

IV. The Shunamite woman:
   A. One of the greatest hospitality stories is found in 2 Kings 4:8-13.

      B. Her hospitality was not for recompense, as she expected nothing in return!

V. Job:

      A. Job 31:32

      B. Do you have open doors when it comes to hospitality?

Conclusion

1. May we learn from these Old Testament people.

2. "And go and do thou likewise" (Luke 10:37)!

~ 50 ~
New Testament Hospitality
1 Peter 4:9

Introduction

1. Being hospitable is no accident. It takes effort, time and money. We are living in a time when hospitality is almost a forgotten word.
2. This study takes a look at some New Testament people who practiced hospitality.

Discussion

I. The good Samaritan:
   A. Luke 10:30-35
   B. Note the words in the story showing he was hospitable.

II. Mary and Martha:
   A. Luke 10:38
   B. Luke 10:42

III. Lydia:
   A. After her conversion, Lydia constrained the men of God (Acts 16:15).
   B. Lydia would not take no for an answer (Acts 16:39-40)!
   C. Many would say, "I don't suppose you want to come over for dinner, do you?"
   D. We need more of Lydia's kind!

IV. Aquila and Priscilla:
   A. Acts 18:1-2
   B. Romans 16:3
V. Publius:
   A. Acts 28:2
   B. Acts 27:7
   C. 1 Peter 3:8
VI. Elders:
   A. A qualification for an elder (1 Timothy 3:2)
   B. Titus 1:8
   C. We need more elders and their wives who set good examples of hospitality (1 Peter 5:3). When elders do not practice hospitality, why should we members do so?
VII. Christians:
   A. Romans 12:13
   B. Hospitality is something Christians should enjoy doing! Do you?

Conclusion

1. May each of us be encouraged to be people of hospitality.
2. 1 Peter 4:9
3. Come and obey the Lord and become a member of hospitality!

~ 51 ~
A Plumb Line

Introduction

1. The Bible mentions a plumb line (Amos 7:7-9).
2. Let's set a plumb line in our midst to see if we are in line with God's standard.

Discussion

I. Our attendance

    A. What the plumb line says:

        1. "But seek ye first the kingdom of God" (Matthew 6:33)

        2. The example of first-century Christians (Acts 2:46; 4:31; 11:26; 20:7)

        3. "Not forsaking the assembling" (Hebrews 10:25)

    B. When the plumb line is set next to my attendance, am I in line?

II. Our attitudes

    A. Attitude, good or bad, is ever showing.

    B. The Bible says, "As he thinketh in his heart, so is he" (Proverbs 23:7).

    C. Reading the plumb line:

        1. Attitudes that promote unity and growth in the local church include lowliness, meekness, longsuffering, forbearance and love (Ephesians 4:2).

        2. Is my attitude in line, or do I need an attitude adjustment?

III. Our treatment of others
   A. A look at the plumb line:
      1. Treat others how I want to be treated (Matthew 7:12)
      2. Love others as self (Matthew 22:39)
      3. Look on the things of others (Philippians 2:4)
      4. Teach others (2 Timothy 2:2)
   B. When it comes to the way I treat others, am I upright?
IV. Our giving
   A. It is possible to rob God (Malachi 3:8).
   B. The plumb line:
      1. Give weekly as prospered (1 Corinthians 16:1-2)
      2. Give sacrificially (2 Corinthians 8:3)
      3. Give bountifully, purposefully and cheerfully (2 Corinthians 9:6-7)
   C. Is my giving in line with what the Bible teaches?
V. Our purity
   A. Looking at the plumb line:
      1. "Blessed are the pure in heart" (Matthew 5:8)
      2. "Keep thyself pure" (1 Timothy 5:22)
      3. "Flee also youthful lusts" (2 Timothy 2:22)
      4. Think on pure things (Philippians 4:8)
   B. Next to the plumb line, how pure are we?
VI. Use of the tongue
   A. The tongue has great power (Proverbs 18:21; James 3:3-6).
   B. The plumb line:
      1. Misuse of the tongue: gossip and talebearing (Leviticus 19:16; Proverbs 26:20-22), lying (Ephesians 4:25), corrupt communication (Ephesians 4:29)

2. Proper use of the tongue: confessing faith in Christ (Acts 8:37), edifiying (Ephesians 4:29), preaching the word (Acts 8:4)
  C. The tongue must be kept with a bridle to be kept plumb (James 1:26).
VII. The family relationship
  A. Let's stretch out the plumb line in several areas of the family:
   1. Our marriage (Genesis 2:18-24; Matthew 19:9; Romans 7:2-3)
   2. Husbands and wives (Ephesians 5:24-33; 1 Peter 3:1-7)
   3. Parents (Proverbs 22:6; Ephesians 6:4; Titus 2:4)
   4. Children (Ephesians 6:1-3; 1 Timothy 5:4)
  B. Are we plumb or are there some changes that need to be made?
VIII. The church
  A. A lot of churches are out of plumb.
  B. Some things to check by the plumb line:
   1. Origin (Ephesians 3:10-11; Acts 2)
   2. Name (Romans 16:16; Acts 11:26)
   3. Work (Ephesians 4:12)
   4. Worship (Acts 2:42; Ephesians 5:19)
   5. Organization (Ephesians 1:21-23; Philippians 1:1)
   6. Doctrine (2 John 9)
  C. Is the church in line with what the Scriptures teach?

Conclusion
1. The word of the Lord is right (Psalm 33:4).
2. May we be in proper alignment with the plumb line!

~ 52 ~
Let Us Rise Up and Build

Introduction

1. This was the answer when Nehemiah sounded the building call (Nehemiah 2:17-18).

2. This lesson takes principles from the building books (Ezra and Nehemiah) and makes spiritual application today. These are a must, if we are to be successful.

Discussion

I. Unity

   A. The rebuilding people were a united people!
      1. Ezra 3:1
      2. Nehemiah 8:1
   B. There is a real need for Christians today to be as one man (John 17:21; 1 Corinthians 1:10; Ephesians 4:1-6).

II. A willing heart

   A. God has always required a willing heart of His people (Exodus 25:2).
   B. The children out of captivity were willing-hearted!
      1. Ezra 1:6
      2. Ezra 2:68-69
      3. Ezra 3:5
   C. We must have a willing heart (2 Corinthians 8:12).

III. A mind to work
   A. This was the key to wall-building success!
      1. Nehemiah 4:6
      2. Accomplished in only 52 days (Nehemiah 6:15)
   B. This was the mind of our Lord (John 9:4).
   C. It must be the mind of every Christian (1 Corinthians 15:58).
IV. "Stick-to-it-iveness"
   A. Opposition could not keep them from getting the job done!
      1. Nehemiah 4
      2. They built, "every one with one of his hands wrought in the work, and with the other hand held a weapon" (v. 17).
   B. We need a good dose of this today (Galatians 6:9)!
V. An uncompromising spirit
   A. The returning builders faced adversaries who said, "Let's compromise!" They refused to give in to their proposals!
      1. Ezra 4:1-3
      2. Nehemiah 6:2-3
   B. We must be uncompromising (Exodus 10:26; Galatians 2:4-5)!
VI. Respect for the divine pattern
   A. The building was done "as it is written."
      1. Ezra 3:2, 4
      2. Nehemiah 6:18; 8:15
   B. Anytime God has called upon man to build, He has given him a pattern by which to build (Genesis 6:14; Exodus 25:8-9, 40; 1 Chronicles 28:11-12, 18-19).
   C. The New Testament is our pattern, and we must build as it is written!
      1. 1 Corinthians 4:6
      2. Colossians 3:17

3. James 1:25
4. 2 John 9

Conclusion

1. There is spiritual building that needs to be done today (Ephesians 4:16; Jude 20).
2. May we apply these principles as we rise up and build!

~ 53 ~
Expressions of Obedience

Introduction

1. God has always called upon man to obey Him.

   a. The keynote of Deuteronomy: obedience (Deuteronomy 10:12-13; 11:27)

   b. Ecclesiastes 12:13

   c. Acts 5:29

   d. Hebrews 5:8-9

   e. Revelation 22:14

2. Down through the ages, obedience to God has been expressed in the lives of men and women. So, we take a look at expressions of obedience.

Discussion

I. "Thus did Noah"

   A. When God commissioned Noah to make an ark, it is said, "Thus did Noah; according to all that God commanded him, so did he" (Genesis 6:22).

   B. Other expressions of obedience in the life of Noah:

      1. "Noah did according unto all that the Lord commanded him" (Genesis 7:5)

      2. "…as God had commanded Noah" (Genesis 7:9)

      3. "…as God had commanded him" (Genesis 7:16)

      4. "By faith Noah…prepared an ark" (Hebrews 11:7)

II. "So Abram departed"

   A. When the Lord called Abram out of Ur of the Chaldees, his obedience is expressed in ten words: "So Abram departed, as the Lord had spoken unto him" (Genesis 12:4).

   B. The Hebrew writer recorded, "By faith Abraham…obeyed" (Hebrews 11:8).

III. "The children of Israel went"

   A. When Israel was given instruction concerning the Lord's Passover, it is written, "And the children of Israel went away, and did as the Lord had commanded Moses and Aaron, so did they" (Exodus 12:28).

   B. Notice Exodus 12:21-23.

IV. "Moses did as the Lord commanded"

   A. Leviticus 8:4

   B. Five other times in Leviticus 8 it is said of Moses that he did "as the Lord commanded" (vv. 9, 13, 17, 21, 29).

V. "Joshua left nothing undone"

   A. Joshua 11:15

   B. What a statement!

   C. The obedience expressed in the life of Joshua had great influence. "And Israel served the Lord all the days of Joshua" (Joshua 24:31).

VI. "Samuel did that which the Lord spake"

   A. 1 Samuel 16:4

   B. The setting finds Samuel being charged by the Lord to anoint a king in place of Saul (1 Samuel 16:1-3).

VII. "The people went forth and made themselves booths"

   A. Nehemiah 8:16

   B. The law of God was read. The people found written in the law that they should make booths. They went and did as commanded in the law.

VIII. "The disciples did as Jesus had appointed them"
  A. Entrance into Jerusalem (Matthew 21:6)
  B. Preparation for the Passover (Matthew 26:19)

Conclusion
1. May it be said of us as it is said of them (Matthew 28:20).
2. Express your obedience right now by doing what the Lord says.

~ 54 ~
Heroic Faith

Introduction

1. Hebrews 11 catalogues great heroes of faith. These were said to have faith because of what they did.
2. If we will do the kind of things they did, then our faith will be heroic.

Discussion

I. An acceptable sacrifice offering faith

    A. Hebrews 11:4

    B. Genesis 4:1-7

    C. We must offer acceptable sacrifices unto God (Romans 12:1; Philippians 4:18; Hebrews 13:15-16; 1 Peter 2:5).

II. A God pleasing faith

    A. Hebrews 11:5

    B. Genesis 5:22-24

    C. We must strive to please God today (Colossians 1:10; 1 Thessalonians 4:1)

III. A warning heeding faith

    A. Hebrews 11:7

    B. God warned Noah, and Noah heeded the warning (Genesis 6:13-22).

- C. We must heed the warnings of God within His word (Ezekiel 33:1-5; Acts 20:31; 1 Corinthians 4:14; Colossians 1:28).

IV. A fear moving faith

- A. Hebrews 11:7
- B. Fear of God is reverence for God that moves us to do the will of God.
- C. We must fear God (Ecclesiastes 12:13; Acts 10:35; Hebrews 12:28).

V. A preparation making faith

- A. Hebrews 11:7
- B. 1 Peter 3:20
- C. We must make preparation (Matthew 24:44).

VI. An obedient faith

- A. Hebrews 11:8
- B. Genesis 12:1-5
- C. We need to have the faith to do what God says, whatever it is (Hebrews 5:9).

VII. A sojourning faith

- A. Hebrews 11:9-10
- B. Genesis 12:8-9; 13:3, 18; 18:1, 9; 23:3-4
- C. We are strangers and pilgrims (1 Peter 2:11).

VIII. A faithful God judging faith

- A. Hebrews 11:11-12
- B. Genesis 17:19; 18:14
- C. We need to have faith that God keeps His promises and nothing is too hard for the Lord!

IX. A trial passing faith

- A. Hebrews 11:17-19
- B. Genesis 22:1-12

      C. Our faith may be tried (1 Peter 1:7). Will our faith pass the test?
X. A refusing faith
      A. Hebrews 11:24
      B. Exodus 2:10-11
      C. We must refuse some things (Isaiah 7:15-16; 1 Timothy 4:7; Genesis 39:8; 1 Corinthians 6:18).
XI. A choosing faith
      A. Hebrews 11:25
      B. Our faith must be a choosing faith (Deuteronomy 30:19; Joshua 24:15; Isaiah 7:15-16).
XII. A forsaking faith
      A. Hebrews 11:27
      B. Exodus 10:28-29
      C. There are some things we must give up (Luke 14:33).
XIII. A keeping faith
      A. Hebrews 11:28
      B. Exodus 12:21
      C. Our faith must lead us to be keepers (1 Corinthians 15:1-2; Ephesians 4:3; John 14:15).
XIV. An enduring faith
      A. Hebrews 11:32-38
      B. Our faith must endure (Matthew 24:13; 2 Thessalonians 1:4; 2 Timothy 2:3)!
XV. A lifelong faith
      A. Hebrews 11:13
      B. We must be faithful unto death (Revelation 2:10).

Conclusion
1. You might like to use this as a personal checklist.
2. Faith is essential to pleasing God (Hebrews 11:6).

~ 55 ~
Soul Winning

Introduction

1. Proverbs 11:30

2. Wise men are soul winners. If we are interested in being wise, we will be interested in soul winning.

Discussion

I. Soul winning songs

   A. One of the ways we teach one another is through singing (Colossians 3:16).

   B. Many of the songs we sing are designed to stimulate us to be soul winners. Some examples:

      1. "Will You Not Tell It Today?"

      2. "You Never Mentioned Him to Me"

      3. "A Soul Winner for Jesus"

II. First century soul winners

   A. Anna (Luke 2:36-38)

   B. Andrew (John 1:40-42)

   C. Jesus (Luke 19:10; John 4)

   D. The woman of Samaria (John 4:28-30, 39)

   E. First church members (Acts 8:4; 11:19-21)

III. Why should I be a soul winner?

   A. To be wise (Proverbs 11:30)

B. To carry out the Great Commission (Mark 16:15-16)

C. The value of a soul (Matthew 16:26)

D. To be like Christ (Matthew 10:25)

E. To do the greatest work that can be done for another (Matthew 7:12)

F. To bring joy (Luke 15:7; Acts 8:39)

G. To save self (1 Timothy 4:16)

IV. Excuses for not winning souls

A. Discuss these:

1. I can't do it.

2. I'm too busy.

3. Nobody will listen.

4. I'm too tired.

5. I'm afraid.

6. I don't know how.

B. When excuses fade away:

1. Realize that men are lost in sin (Romans 3:23).

2. The wages of sin is death (Romans 6:23).

3. The gospel is the only remedy (Romans 1:16).

4. Christ has no hands but our hands to do His work today!

V. Soul winning prospects

A. Look on the fields (John 4:35)

B. Consider these:

1. Those already attending

2. Those you work with

3. Relatives and friends of members

4. New residents

5. Members no longer attending

C. Make a list of six people you know who need the gospel. Pick one and go to it!

VI. Soul winning tools

A. Every trade has its tools!

B. Some tools for the soul winner:

1. The Bible
2. Invitations
3. Tracts
4. Correspondence course
5. Home Bible study

C. Tools are of no value unless they are used!

Conclusion

1. The early church grew as it was made up of soul winners (Acts 2:47; 5:41-42).
2. If we want to be wise and see the church grow, then we must get the seed out of the barn (Haggai 2:19) and put it in the soil (Luke 8:5-15)!

~ 56 ~
Why Stop the Chariot?

Introduction

1. Acts 8:26-39

2. Verse 38: "And he commanded the chariot to stand still..." makes some things stand out.

Discussion

I. If some things men say be true, why stop the chariot?

   A. A number of things men say today, if true, make it entirely unnecessary for the Ethiopian to stop the chariot.

   B. Consider some examples:

      1. If being an honest and good person is all that is required (v. 27)
      2. If being religious is all it takes (v. 27)
      3. If just reading the Scriptures is enough to be saved (vv. 28-34)
      4. If just hearing preaching is enough (v. 35)
      5. If justified by faith only (v. 37)
      6. If saved by praying "the sinner's prayer"
      7. If baptism is not essential to salvation
      8. If sprinkling or pouring is sufficient

II. Why you need to stop the chariot

   A. The shortness and uncertainty of your life (James 4:14)

- B. The value of your soul (Matthew 16:26)
- C. Judgment is coming (Acts 24:25)
- D. You must obey the Lord to be saved (Matthew 7:21; Hebrews 5:9)

III. You are the one who must stop the chariot.
- A. Notice who stopped the chariot: the Ethiopian (vv. 37-38).
- B. Obeying the gospel is an individual decision *you* must make!

IV. When to stop the chariot
- A. Observe when he stopped the chariot: when he heard the gospel, believed it, and recognized his need to obey it (vv. 35-38).
- B. Now is the time to stop the chariot (2 Corinthians 6:2).

Conclusion

1. We encourage you to stop the chariot right now and obey the gospel.
2. If you have obeyed the gospel and your chariot has taken a wrong turn, we plead with you to get back on track through repentance and prayer.

~ 57 ~
Six Houses

Introduction

1. The word "house" appears more than 2,000 times throughout the word of God.
2. It is used different ways, depending on the context.
3. This study brings to our attention six different houses mentioned in the Bible.

Discussion

I. The family

    A. This is the first way the word "house" is used in the scriptures.

    B. God told Noah, "Come thou and all thy house into the ark (Genesis 7:1).

    C. "By faith Noah, being warned of God of things not seen as yet, moved with fear, prepared an ark to the saving of his house" (Hebrews 11:7).

    D. Cornelius "feared God with all his house" (Acts 10:2).

    E. Three things about this house:

        1. It is God-instituted (Genesis 2:18-24).

        2. It is man-headed and woman-subjected (Genesis 3:16; Ephesians 5:22-33).

        3. It is the child-rearing place (Genesis 1:28; Ephesians 6:4).

II. A dwelling place

    A. "And Jacob journeyed to Succoth, and built him an house, and

made booths for his cattle" (Genesis 33:17).
- B. Some things the Bible teaches about this house:
    1. A place for practicing hospitality:
        a. Lot (Genesis 19:2-4, 10-11)
        b. Rebekah and Laban (Genesis 24:23, 31-32)
    2. A place for teaching:
        a. Deuteronomy 6:7-9; 11:19-21
        b. Acts 5:42; 20:20
    3. A place for eating and drinking:
        a. Acts 2:46
        b. 1 Corinthians 11:22, 34
- C. Haggai finds the Lord's people putting too much emphasis on this house, and not enough attention being given to the Lord's house (Haggai 1:2, 4, 9).

III. The Old Testament temple
- A. It came into David's heart to build a house for God (2 Samuel 7:2, 7).
- B. It was built and dedicated by Solomon (1 Kings 4-8).
- C. It was the place where Jews assembled for worship (Deuteronomy 16).

IV. The physical body
- A. 2 Corinthians 5:1
- B. Ecclesiastes 12:3
- C. The physical body houses the spirit (Zechariah 12:1; James 2:26).
- D. We need to take care of it and glorify God in it (1 Corinthians 6:18-20).

V. The New Testament church
- A. 1 Timothy 3:15
- B. Hebrews 3:6

- C. Ephesians 2:19
- D. A spiritual house (1 Peter 2:5)
- E. It is God-planned (Ephesians 3:10-11), Christ-built (Matthew 16:18), blood-purchased (Acts 20:28), Christ-headed (Ephesians 1:20-23), and heaven-bound (1 Corinthians 15:24).

VI. This meeting house

- A. Authority for it (Hebrews 10:25)
- B. Use of it:
    1. Worshipping God (Acts 2:42; Ephesians 5:19)
    2. Doing the work of the Lord (Ephesians 4:12; 1 Timothy 3:15)

Conclusion

1. We invite you to become a part of God's house today, the New Testament church, and to work and worship with us in this house.
2. Come as we sing!

~ 58 ~
Accessing God's Grace

Introduction

1. Romans 5:1-2
2. The scriptures often talk about God's grace.
   a. Appeared to all (Titus 2:11; Hebrews 2:9)
   b. Justifies (Romans 3:24; Titus 3:7)
   c. Saves (Ephesians 2:5, 8)
3. Just because God's grace has appeared does not mean we are saved.
   a. We must access this grace (Romans 5:2).
   b. We access God's grace by faith. The faith by which we access God's grace is the faith that obeys (Romans 1:5; 16:26; Hebrews 5:8-9).
4. Notice some examples of accessing God's grace:

Discussion

I. Noah
   A. Genesis 6:8
   B. God gave Noah instruction as to what he was to do (Genesis 6:14-21).
   C. Noah accessed God's grace by faith when he built the ark with the materials God specified, according to the dimensions given by God, and took everything that God said into the ark (Genesis 6:22; 7:5; Hebrews 11:7).

II. The children of Israel
   A. In the healing of those bitten by snakes
      1. Numbers 21:4-9
      2. When they were bitten, if they had faith in God, they did what God said and had access into the grace of God (they lived).
   B. In the gift of Jericho
      1. Joshua 6:1-20
      2. God gave instruction concerning what they were to do (vv. 3-5).
      3. They obeyed and took the city (vv. 12-16, 20).
      4. When they did what God said, they accessed God's grace and the walls fell (Hebrews 11:30).

III. Naaman
   A. 2 Kings 5:1-14
   B. Naaman was given instruction as to what he was to do (v. 10).
   C. God cleansed him of his leprosy when he had enough faith to do what he was instructed to do (v. 14).

IV. Men today
   A. Some examples of folks in New Testament days who accessed God's grace:
      1. Those on Pentecost (Acts 2). When they repented and were baptized, they accessed God's grace—the remission of sins!
      2. Saul of Tarsus (Acts 9; 22; 26; 1 Corinthians 15:10). When he went into the city as the Lord said and did what the man of God said do, was baptized, he by faith accessed God's grace—his sins were washed away!
      3. The Corinthians (1 Corinthians 6:9-11; Romans 3:24; 1 Corinthians 1:4). The Corinthians accessed God's grace—washed, sanctified, justified—when they, "hearing believed, and were baptized" (Acts 18:8).

4. The Ephesians (Ephesians 1:7; 2). How were the Ephesians saved by grace? They accessed God's grace when they obeyed the Lord in being baptized in the name of the Lord (Acts 19:5).

B. Once we access God's grace, we must stand in His grace (Romans 5:2; 1 Peter 5:12).

1. It's possible to fall from grace (Galatians 5:4), fail of God's grace (Hebrews 12:15), and receive the grace of God in vain (2 Corinthians 6:1).

2. We continue in God's grace (Acts 13:43) as we continue in His law, doing what His word says (James 1:25).

Conclusion

1. Express your faith in obedience to the will of God today so that you can access God's grace.

2. If you've accessed God's grace but have failed and fallen, repent and pray so you can be restored to God's favor (Acts 8:22).

~ 59 ~
I Am Resolved

Introduction

1. With a new year just around the bend, a lot of folks are making New Year's resolutions. It's a good time to resolve to do some things of a spiritual nature.

2. In the parable of the unjust steward, the man said, "I am resolved" (Luke 16:4). May I suggest some things you may want to resolve to do? I am resolved:

Discussion

I. To be a Christian
   A. Acts 11:26; 26:28
   B. 1 Peter 4:16

II. To be restored
   A. Galatians 6:1
   B. James 5:19-20

III. To be at every service
   A. Matthew 6:33
   B. Because the Lord wants me to be (Hebrews 10:25), and I want to be (Psalm 122:1)

IV. To read my Bible every day
   A. Acts 17:11
   B. To know (John 8:32), to not be misled (Acts 20:30), and to grow (1 Peter 2:2)

V. To pray always
   A. Luke 18:1
   B. 1 Thessalonians 5:17
VI. To win one to the Lord
   A. Proverbs 11:30
   B. Like Andrew (John 1:40-42)
VII. To be given to hospitality
   A. Romans 12:13
   B. 1 Peter 4:9
VIII. To go to Heaven
   A. The prepared place for prepared people (John 14:1-3)
   B. And not let anyone or anything keep me out (Revelation 22:14)

Conclusion

1. "Resolved" means firmly determined to do something.
2. Come as we sing!

~ 60 ~
Some Things Jesus Did Not Do

Introduction

1. There are a lot of misconceptions about Jesus.
2. This study makes us aware of some things Jesus did not do.

Discussion

I. Give up His deity

    A. Some have said that when Jesus came to earth He gave up His deity and became just an ordinary man like you and me. He did not!

    B. The Bible teaches Jesus was both "the Son of man" (Mark 14:41) and "the Son of God" (Mark 1:1). He was 100% man and 100% God while on earth!

II. Commit sin

    A. Hebrews 4:15

    B. 1 Peter 2:22

III. Make Himself of reputation

    A. Philippians 2:7

    B. Mark 10:45

IV. Retaliate

    A. Some, when mistreated, get even. Not Jesus!

    B. 1 Peter 2:23

V. Tolerate error or overlook sin

A. John 2:16

   B. Matthew 9:2

   C. John 8:11

VI. Build more than one church

   A. Join the church of your choice is the plea of the day!

   B. The Lord only built one church—His (Matthew 16:18).

   C. There is one body (Ephesians 4:4), which is the church (Colossians 1:24).

VII. Please Himself

   A. Luke 22:42

   B. Hebrews 10:9

   C. Romans 15:3

   D. John 8:29

VIII. Teach one thing and practice another

   A. Acts 1:1

   B. Some examples: Jesus loved (John 15:13) and taught love (John 13:34-35); He forgave (Luke 23:34) and taught forgiveness (Matthew 6:14-15).

IX. Apologize for His teaching

   A. Some think they have to apologize for the truth.

   B. The Lord didn't. Observe Matthew 15:12-14.

X. Come down from the cross

   A. He was taunted, "Come down" (Matthew 27:40).

   B. He could have come down (Matthew 26:53).

   C. He stayed on the cross for you and me (Hebrews 2:9).

XI. Stay in the grave

   A. Matthew 28:6

   B. Acts 2:27

   C. Many things are made possible by the resurrection of Jesus!

XII. Return invisibly

    A. Some have tried to convince us the Lord has already returned—just no one saw Him! Not so!

    B. His coming will be audible (1 Corinthians 15:52) and visible (Revelation 1:7).

    C. Since He is yet to come, there is still the need to "be ready" (Matthew 24:44).

Conclusion

1. A good companion sermon is "Some Things Jesus Did."
2. You are invited to come to Jesus (Matthew 11:28-30).

~ 61 ~
Some Things Jesus Did

Introduction

1. John 21:25
2. To impress us with who Jesus is, we call attention to some things Jesus did.

Discussion

I. Obeyed His parents

    A. Luke 2:51

    B. A need for children to do this today (Ephesians 6:1)

II. Was baptized

    A. Luke 3:21

    B. It was to "fulfil all righteousness" (Matthew 3:15).

    C. It was an immersion (Matthew 3:16).

III. Resisted the devil

    A. Luke 4:1-13

    B. By recalling scripture (vv. 4, 8, 12; Psalm 119:11).

IV. Taught and preached

    A. Luke 4:15, 32

    B. Luke 8:1

    C. He is the master teacher/preacher!

Sermons for the Seed Sower

V. Read the scriptures
    A. Luke 4:16
    B. Much emphasis is placed on this (1 Timothy 4:13; Ephesians 4:3; Revelation 1:3).

VI. Fulfilled scriptures
    A. Isaiah 61:1-2
    B. Luke 4:21
    C. Matthew 1:22
    D. Luke 24:44

VII. Performed miracles
    A. He cast out devils (Luke 4:35).
    B. He healed the sick (Luke 4:38-40).
    C. He raised the dead (Luke 7:11-15; John 11:43-44).
    D. He calmed the storm (Luke 8:23-24).
    E. He fed five thousand (Luke 9:12-17).

VIII. Prayed
    A. Luke 5:16
    B. Luke 6:12

IX. Forgave sins
    A. Luke 5:20-24
    B. Luke 7:48

X. Gave thanks
    A. John 6:11
    B. Matthew 26:27

XI. Wept
    A. Luke 19:41
    B. John 11:35

XII. Forgave His enemies
    A. Luke 23:34

B. He exemplified Matthew 5:44.

XIII. Set a good example

    A. John 13:15

    B. 1 Peter 2:21

XIV. Died, was buried, arose, appeared and ascended

    A. Luke 23-24

    B. 1 Corinthians 15:1-8

XV. Promised to come again

    A. John 14:1-3

    B. He will come as He left (Acts 1:9-11).

    C. He will come as a thief (2 Peter 3:10).

Conclusion

1. John 20:30-31
2. We invite you to come to Jesus today!

~ 62 ~
What Paul Told the Ephesians About the Church

Introduction

1. Ephesians is God's church letter. The word "church" occurs 9 times and the word "body" with reference to the church appears 9 times within the book.

2. Let's learn what Paul told the Ephesians about the church.

Discussion

I. The church is headed by Christ

   A. The church is not headed by some man or group of men.

   B. Christ is the head!

   1. Ephesians 1:22

   2. Ephesians 4:15

   3. Ephesians 5:23

II. The church is the body of Christ

   A. Ephesians 1:22-23

   B. There is one body (Ephesians 4:4). Thus, one church.

   C. This is the realm of the reconciled (Ephesians 2:16) and the sphere of the saved (Ephesians 5:23).

III. The church is the fulness of Christ

   A. Ephesians 1:23

    B. Thus, whatever is available in Christ cannot be found outside the church!

IV. The church is according to God's eternal purpose
    A. Ephesians 3:10-11
    B. The church was not an afterthought or here by accident, it was planned by God from the beginning!

V. The church gives glory unto God
    A. Ephesians 3:21
    B. Some think the church must get the glory. No, glory is given unto God in the church by Christ!

VI. The church is all-sufficient
    A. Ephesians 4:11-16
    B. The Lord has equipped the church with everything needed to do everything He has commanded.

VII. The church is subject unto Christ
    A. Ephesians 5:24
    B. The relationship between Christ and the church demands that the church be under the authority of Christ.

VIII. The church is loved by Christ
    A. Ephesians 5:25
    B. The fact that Christ gave Himself for the church shows the real importance of the church.

IX. The church is to be a glorious church
    A. Ephesians 5:27
    B. Let us not be guilty of blemishing the bride of Christ!

X. Christ and the church go together
    A. Ephesians 5:32
    B. They are joined by that word "and." You can't have one without the other!

Conclusion

1. May we respect everything the Bible says about the church.
2. You are invited to become a member of the church now as we sing.

~ 63 ~
What Paul Told the Colossians About Christ

Introduction

1. Ephesians and Colossians are companion books. As Ephesians emphasizes the church, Colossians centers around Christ.
2. Be impressed with some things Paul told the Colossians about Christ.

Discussion

I. Christ is Lord

   A. Colossians 1:2-3

   B. As Lord, Christ is the One to whom we belong; He is our Master.

   C. Christ is not a lord among lords, but "Lord of lords" (1 Timothy 6:14-15).

II. Christ is the Son of God

   A. "God and the Father of our Lord Jesus Christ" (Colossians 1:3)

   B. "His dear Son" (Colossians 1:13)

   C. The Father said of Jesus, "This is my beloved Son" (Matthew 17:5).

   D. "God…hath in these last days spoken unto us by His Son" (Hebrews 1:1-2).

   E. As the Son of God, Christ is divine in nature.

III. Christ is king
   A. "The kingdom of his dear Son" (Colossians 1:13)
   B. Four things necessary for a kingdom:
      1. A king: Christ is "King of kings" (1 Timothy 6:14-15).
      2. Subjects: Those "translated into the kingdom" are the subjects (Colossians 1:13).
      3. Territory: "All the world" is the territory of the kingdom (Mark 16:15-16).
      4. Law: The "law of Christ" is the law of the kingdom (Galatians 6:2).
   C. The kingdom of Christ is the church of Christ (Colossians 1:13, 22, 24).

IV. Christ is redeemer
   A. "In whom we have redemption" (Colossians 1:14)
   B. Redemption is the forgiveness of sins and is made possible through the blood of Christ.

V. Christ is the image of the invisible God
   A. "Who is the image of the invisible God" (Colossians 1:15)
   B. God is invisible.
      1. No man hath seen God (John 1:18; 1 John 4:12).
      2. God is a Spirit (John 4:24).
      3. Hebrews 11:27 speaks of "him who is invisible."
   C. Christ, the image of God, is the likeness of God.
      1. Christ, who is the image of God (2 Corinthians 4:4)
      2. The express image of His person (Hebrews 1:3)
      3. He that hath seen me hath seen the Father (John 14:9)
   D. The Christian is "conformed to the image of" Christ (Romans 8:29).

VI. Christ is the firstborn of every creature
   A. Colossians 1:15

B. The firstborn among the Hebrews had distinctions, honor and privilege.

C. Christ holds the most elevated position above all others. The reason is found in verses 16 and 17.

VII. Christ is the agent of creation

A. "For by him were all things created" (Colossians 1:16).

B. John 1:3

C. Hebrews 1:2

VIII. Christ is eternal

A. "He is before all things" (Colossians 1:17).

B. This affirms His preexistence.

1. He was in the beginning with God (John 1:1).

2. He was before Abraham (John 8:58).

IX. Christ is head of the church

A. Colossians 1:18

B. He has all authority and rule over His church (Ephesians 1:22-23; 5:23).

X. Christ is firstborn from the dead

A. Colossians 1:18

B. This is a reference to His resurrection from the dead. He was not the first to rise from the dead, but the first who rose to die no more.

XI. Christ is the one in whom all fulness dwells

A. Colossians 1:19; 2:9

B. Fulness means completeness.

C. Thus, He has all the attributes or completeness of deity. He is fully God.

XII. Christ is reconciler

A. Colossians 1:20-23

B. Notice what they were and what they became.

C. This change occurred through the blood of His cross, in the body (vv. 20, 22).

D. It is conditional: "If" (v. 23).

Conclusion

1. Christ is the preeminent One (Colossians 1:18), and we are complete in Him (Colossians 2:10).

2. Come to Christ today!

~ 64 ~
Reading and Understanding the Bible

Introduction

1. Many think the Bible cannot be understood. The Bible makes the claim that it can be read and understood (Ephesians 3:3-5; 5:17).

2. Some principles to help us in reading and understanding the Bible:

Discussion

I. Read it as it is

   A. 1 Thessalonians 2:13

   B. Not as the word of men, but the word of God

      1. Galatians 1:11-12

      2. 1 Corinthians 11:23; 14:37

      3. 2 Timothy 3:16

      4. 1 Corinthians 2:13

      5. 2 Peter 1:21

II. Read it with a prepared heart

   A. James 1:21

   B. Heart = soil and word = seed (Luke 8:5-11)

   C. Ezra 7:10

   D. Prepared to do what it says (James 1:22-25; John 7:17)

III. Read everything it says on a subject

   A. Psalm 119:160; 139:17

B. A partial view is often an inaccurate and dangerous view. Remember the blind men and the elephant?

C. Faith is an example (Romans 5:1). Read James 2:24.

IV. Read the context

A. The context may be a few verses, a chapter, or a whole book.

B. Much error is taught by stringing verses together out of context.

C. Examples of reading the context:

1. John 6:44
2. Romans 10:13

V. Read considering who is speaking and who is being spoken to

A. Who is speaking (Genesis 3:4; Job)

B. Who is being spoken to (John 14:26; Galatians 6:10; James 1:27)

VI. Read realizing one verse can only teach what another verse will allow it

A. Truth is harmonious!

B. Note some examples:

1. Romans 10:13 and Matthew 7:21
2. Romans 5:1 and James 2:24
3. Romans 14 and 2 John 9-11

VII. Read recognizing figurative language

A. Understand figurative passages figuratively and literal passages literally.

B. Notice some examples.

Conclusion

1. May we apply these principles as we read so as to understand (Colossians 1:9).

2. We urge you to do what the Bible teaches.

~ 65 ~
Is It Too Much for You?

Introduction

1. Jeroboam, king of Israel, made two calves of gold, set one in Bethel and the other in Dan, and convinced the Lord's people it was too much for them to go up to Jerusalem (1 Kings 12:26-30).

2. In light of that, I'm asking the question, "Is it too much for you?"

Discussion

I. To pray daily

   A. Matthew 6:11

   B. Luke 18:1

   C. 1 Thessalonians 5:17

   D. Daniel 6:10

   E. Psalm 55:17

II. To read your Bible every day

   A. 1 Timothy 4:13

   B. Revelation 1:3

   C. Ephesians 3:4

   D. Acts 17:11

III. To attend the services of the church faithfully

   A. Acts 2:46

   B. Acts 4:31

   C. Acts 11:26

- D. Acts 20:7
- E. Hebrews 10:25
- F. Matthew 6:33

IV. To give as you've prospered
- A. 1 Corinthians 16:1-2
- B. 2 Corinthians 9:6-7

V. To supply your part
- A. Ephesians 4:16
- B. Mark 14:8

VI. To practice hospitality
- A. Romans 12:13
- B. 1 Peter 4:9
- C. Hebrews 13:2
- D. Genesis 18:1-6
- E. 2 Kings 4:8-10

VII. To visit
- A. James 1:27
- B. Acts 15:36
- C. Matthew 25:31-46

VIII. To teach others
- A. John 6:44-45
- B. Matthew 28:19-20
- C. 2 Timothy 2:2

IX. To bring back the wandering
- A. Luke 15:4-7
- B. Galatians 6:1
- C. James 5:19-20

X. To be what God would have you be in the home
   A. As a child (Ephesians 6:1-3)
   B. As a husband (Ephesians 5:25, 28-29, 33; 1 Peter 3:7)
   C. As a wife (Titus 2:4; Ephesians 5:22-24, 33; 1 Peter 3:5-6)
   D. As a parent (Proverbs 22:6; 13:24; 22:15; 23:13-14; 29:15; Ephesians 6:4)
XI. To forgive those who sin against you
   A. Matthew 6:14-15
   B. Matthew 18:21-35
   C. Colossians 3:13
XII. To obey the gospel
   A. Hebrews 5:9
   B. 2 Thessalonians 1:9
XIII. To be faithful
   A. Revelation 2:10
   B. 1 Corinthians 15:58
   C. Titus 2:12

Conclusion

1. It was not too much for God to give His Son or for the Son to give His life.
2. May it not be too much for us to fear God and keep His commandments!

~ 66 ~
I of _____

Introduction

1. 1 Corinthians 1:10-15

2. This teaching shows division is contrary to the will of God, and it is wrong to wear the names of men.

3. Whose are you? Who do you belong to? Two things are necessary to put Christ in the blank.

Discussion

I. Was Christ crucified for you?

  A. Acts 2:23

  B. 1 Corinthians 2:2

  C. John 19

  D. Hebrews 2:9

  E. Romans 5:8

  F. 1 John 2:2

  G. 1 Timothy 2:6

II. Were you baptized in the name of Christ?

  A. By the authority of Christ (Matthew 28:18-19)

  B. Being taught the gospel of Christ (Matthew 28:19; Mark 16:15; Acts 8:12)

  C. Believing in Christ and the gospel (Mark 16:16; Acts 8:37)

  D. Repenting as commanded by Christ (Luke 13:3; Acts 2:38)

E. Confessing faith in Christ (Acts 8:37)

F. By immersion (Acts 8:36-38; Romans 6:4-5)

G. For the remission of sins (Acts 2:38)

H. Into Christ and His body (Galatians 3:27; 1 Corinthians 12:13)

Conclusion

1. The fact that Paul had not been crucified for the Corinthians and they had not been baptized in the name of Paul exposed the error of wearing Paul's name.

2. However, just because the Lord has been crucified for us does not mean we are of Christ. We must be baptized in the name of Christ to belong to Christ.

~ 67 ~
Principles to Help Us Prevail

Introduction

1. Judges 6-7

2. This study takes principles from Israel's defeat of the Midianite people to help us prevail spiritually.

Discussion

I. Turn to the Lord

   A. The Lord's people were oppressed by Midian because they had left the Lord (Judges 6:1-6, 10).

   B. They were made to prevail because they turned to the Lord (Judges 6:6-7).

   C. If we are to prevail, we must turn unto the Lord!

II. Be as one man

   A. Judges 6:16

   B. If we are to be successful, we must be as one man!

      1. Psalm 133

      2. Matthew 12:25

      3. John 17:20-21

      4. Romans 16:17

      5. 1 Corinthians 1:10

      6. Ephesians 4:3-6

III. Recognize there is no restraint to the Lord to save by many or by few
   A. 1 Samuel 14:6
   B. This is illustrated in the Lord's people prevailing over the Midianites.
      1. The Midianites were like grasshoppers for multitude (Judges 7:12).
      2. The Lord would bring deliverance by 300 men (Judges 7:1-7). One might ask, "what are they among so many" (John 6:9)?
   C. The Lord was on their side (Leviticus 26:8)!
   D. Never underestimate what can be accomplished by few!

IV. Realize the foolishness of God is wiser than men
   A. 1 Corinthians 1:18-25
   B. As seen in this story:
      1. To reduce the army from 32,000 to 300 (Judges 7:3-6)
      2. To go armed with a trumpet, empty pitcher, and lamp (Judges 7:16)
      3. It worked (Judges 7:19-21)!
   C. God's way is best, even though it may seem foolish to some (Isaiah 55:8-9)!

V. Have good leadership
   A. The people had good, strong leadership in Gideon.
      1. He was a good example (Judges 7:17; Hebrews 11:32).
      2. Too many say, "Don't do as I do. Do as I say." That won't work!
   B. The Lord has provided us with good leadership in well-qualified elders (1 Peter 5:1-3; Hebrews 13:7, 17).

VI. Every man stand in his place
   A. Judges 7:21
   B. The key to their prevailing is that every man stood in his place!

C. We must find our place, get in that place, and stay in our proper place so as to prevail!

D. Discuss the place of these:
   1. Evangelists
   2. Elders
   3. Deacons
   4. Bible class teachers
   5. Men
   6. Women
   7. Children

Conclusion

1. May we make spiritual application of these principles so as to prevail and be spiritually successful today.
2. Turn unto the Lord today!

~ 68 ~
Learning from the Conquest of Jericho

Introduction

1. Romans 15:4

2. This study calls our attention to some spiritual lessons to be learned from Israel's conquest of Jericho (Joshua 6-7; Hebrews 11:30-31; James 2:25).

Discussion

I. A gift may have conditions attached to it

   A. Jericho was God's gift (Joshua 6:2).

   B. There were conditions to be met to take possession of it (Joshua 6:3-5).

   C. Eternal life is the gift of God (Romans 6:23), and there are conditions that must be met to obtain it (HBRCBF).

II. The foolishness of God is wiser than men

   A. 1 Corinthians 1:25

   B. A military leader would think such a strategy for taking a city to be a bunch of foolishness (Joshua 6:3-5)!

   C. It worked (Joshua 6:6-16, 20)!

III. The nature of faith

   A. Hebrews 11:30

   B. They were said to have faith because of what they did. Their faith led them to do what God said!

IV. God is able to do great and mighty things
   A. Jeremiah 33:3
   B. Deuteronomy 9:1-3
   C. God is all-powerful, and there is no end to what He is able to do as seen from this simple story.

V. The need to do exactly as God says
   A. Joshua 6:18-19
   B. Joshua 7:1-11

VI. God is both good and severe
   A. Romans 11:22
   B. His goodness in saving Rahab (Joshua 6:25; Hebrews 11:31; James 2:25) and giving Jericho to Israel.
   C. His severity in the death of Achan (Joshua 7:25) and destroying Jericho for their iniquities.

Conclusion

1. Won't you put your faith to work in obedience to the Lord?
2. Come as we sing!

~ 69 ~
What I Owe the Local Church

Introduction

1. In New Testament days, Christians joined themselves with the faithful church of Christ in their area (Acts 2:42-47; 9:26-28; 11:25-26; 18:24-28).

2. As a member of the local church, I should feel a sense of responsibility to the church of which I am a member. There are some things I owe the local church.

Discussion

I. My faithful attendance

   A. In the first century, Christians assembled together (Acts 4:31; 11:26; 14:27; 20:7-8; 1 Corinthians 5:4; 11:17-18; 14:23, 26).

   B. We are commanded, "Not forsaking the assembling of ourselves together" (Hebrews 10:25).

   C. What faithful attendance is not:

      1. Attending only on Sunday morning

      2. Attending more often than I am absent

      3. Attending only when there is no conflict (family gathering, work, sports and recreation). We are to put the church before everything else (Matthew 6:33).

   D. What does it say to visitors when members are not present when the church is assembled?

II. My financial support

A. The church has financial responsibilities it must meet (expenses in providing an assembling place, evangelism, edification and benevolence).

B. The only authorized way the church has to meet these responsibilities is by the freewill offerings of its members (1 Corinthians 16:1-2).

C. Divine principles governing my financial support:
1. I am to give (1 Corinthians 16:2; 2 Corinthians 9:7).
2. I am to give weekly (1 Corinthians 16:2).
3. I am to give as God hath prospered me (1 Corinthians 16:2).
4. I am to give bountifully (2 Corinthians 9:6).
5. I am to give sacrificially (2 Samuel 24:24; Mark 12:41-44).
6. I am to give cheerfully (2 Corinthians 9:7).

III. My good influence

A. As saints, members of the church are to be people of good influence (1 Corinthians 1:2; 1 Peter 2:9; Ephesians 5:3).

B. Passages which speak of my influence:
1. Matthew 5:13-16
2. 2 Corinthians 3:2
3. Philippians 2:15
4. 1 Timothy 4:12

C. What kind of influence are we having? Are we attracting folks to the church or are we turning people away from it, by our influence?

IV. My involvement in its work

A. The Lord has always had work for His people to do. Adam had a garden to dress and keep (Genesis 2:15). Noah had an ark to build (Genesis 6:14). Moses had people to deliver (Exodus 3:10) and was to show Israel "the work that they must do" (Exodus 18:20). And on that goes!

- B. As the vineyard of the Lord, the church is a workplace (Matthew 20:1).
    1. As a member, I must do my share (Ephesians 4:16).
    2. There are work schedules and work groups I need to be involved in. There is the work of an evangelist (2 Timothy 4:5), the work of bishops and deacons (1 Timothy 3:1-13). I should feel a sense of responsibility to step up and serve as I am able.
    3. 1 Corinthians 15:58
- C. Let's be like the Jerusalem wall-builders who had "a mind to work" (Nehemiah 4:6).

V. My participation in its worship
- A. John 4:24
- B. Worship is not to be viewed as a spectator sport.
- C. Every member is to be a participant in the worship.
    1. Singing (Ephesians 5:19; Colossians 3:16; Hebrews 2:12)
    2. Praying (1 Corinthians 14:15)
    3. Preaching (Luke 4:20; Acts 17:11)
    4. Giving (1 Corinthians 16:1-2)
    5. Observing the Lord's supper (1 Corinthians 11:23-29)
- D. Male members should feel a sense of responsibility to step forward and take part in leading in the worship services.

VI. My care and concern
- A. 1 Corinthians 12:25
- B. Too many are indifferent, apathetic and pass by (Lamentations 1:12; Luke 10:30-32).
- C. Bear burdens (Galatians 6:2)
- D. Warn the unruly, comfort the feebleminded, support the weak (1 Thessalonians 5:14)
- E. Practice hospitality (2 Kings 4:13; 1 Peter 4:9)
- F. Distribute to the necessity of saints (Romans 12:13; Acts 2:45)

Conclusion

1. Christ "loved the church, and gave himself for it" (Ephesians 5:25). He purchased it with His own blood (Acts 20:28). We ought to feel a sense of obligation to it!

2. Become a member of the church today!

~ 70 ~
Going the Way of All the Earth

Introduction

1. Two great men of God spoke of going the way of all the earth:
   1. Joshua (Joshua 23:1, 14)
   2. King David (1 Kings 2:1-4)
2. Going the way of all the earth is an expression of physical death, and there are six things I call to our attention about it.

Discussion

I. We are sure to go
   A. These words may be said by each of us.
   B. Death is sure!
      1. It is recorded concerning the generations of Adam, "And he died" (Genesis 5:5, 8, 11, 14, 17, 20, 27, 32).
      2. Job 30:23
      3. Psalm 89:48
      4. Ecclesiastes 9:5
      5. 1 Corinthians 15:22
      6. Hebrews 9:27

II. It won't be very long until we go
   A. How long do you plan to live?
   B. "Remember how short my time is" (Psalm 89:47).

1. As a flower (Job 14:1-2; Psalm 103:15-16)
2. As a shadow (Job 14:2; 1 Chronicles 29:15)
3. As wind (Job 7:7; Psalm 78:39)
4. As a post (Job 9:25)
5. As the swift ships (Job 9:26)
6. As the eagle (Job 9:26)
7. As a tale that is told (Psalm 90:9)
8. As a weaver's shuttle (Job 7:6)
9. As a vapour (Jas. 4:14)

C. Psalm 90:10, 12

III. What happens when we go

A. Man is composed of "spirit and soul and body" (1 Thessalonians 5:23).
   1. Genesis 2:7; 3:19; 18:27
   2. Zechariah 12:1

B. All that will happen is our soul or spirit will depart our body. The body will go back to the dust from whence it came and our spirit unto God who gave it.
   1. James 2:26
   2. Ecclesiastes 12:1-7

IV. How we can go

A. We can choose how we will go.

B. Two ways we can go:
   1. In our sins (John 8:24)
   2. In Christ (Revelation 14:13)

C. What will be our spiritual condition when we go?

V. Once we go, there's no return

A. There is finality to death as it brings an end to one's earthly existence.

- B. There's no return to this earthly life.
    1. 2 Samuel 14:14
    2. Job 14:11-12
    3. Job 16:22
    4. Psalm 78:39
    5. 2 Samuel 12:23
    6. Luke 16:19-31

VI. We know not when we will go
- A. We have no way of knowing what tomorrow's obituary list will be!
    1. Ecclesiastes 8:6-8
    2. Ecclesiastes 9:12
    3. Proverbs 27:1
    4. Luke 12:19-20
- B. Thus, we must be ready!

Conclusion

1. "Set thine house in order; for thou shalt die, and not live" (2 Kings 20:1).
2. Prepare now by obeying the gospel and being faithful!

~ 71 ~
Behold, He Cometh With Clouds

Introduction

1. Revelation 1:7

2. The Scriptures connect the end with the day of Christ's second coming (1 Corinthians 1:7-8; 15:23-24). Let's find out what the Bible reveals about this event.

Discussion

I. The fact of His coming

   A. The fact that Jesus is coming again is upheld from Matthew through Revelation.

      1. Jesus affirmed He is coming (John 14:3).

      2. Angels announced He is coming (Acts 1:9-11).

      3. Apostles asserted He is coming (2 Thessalonians 1:7, 10; Hebrews 9:28; 2 Peter 3:10).

   B. To reject the fact that Christ is coming is to reject the New Testament!

II. The time of His coming

   A. It is unknown to man.

      1. Matthew 24:36-39, 42-51

      2. Mark 13:32-37

      3. Luke 12:35-48

      4. The parable of the virgins (Matthew 25:1-13)

B. Thus, be ready!

III. The manner of His coming

    A. He will come as He left (Acts 1:9-11).

    B. It will be audible (1 Thessalonians 4:16).

    C. It will be visible (Revelation 1:7).

IV. When He cometh

    A. The dead will be raised (1 Thessalonians 4:13-18).

    B. The living will be changed (1 Corinthians 15:51-52).

    C. The present world will end (2 Peter 3:10-12).

    D. All will be judged and rewarded (Matthew 25:31-46; 2 Timothy 4:1; Matthew 16:27; Revelation 22:12).

    E. The kingdom will be delivered up (1 Corinthians 15:24).

    F. The reign of Christ will end (1 Corinthians 15:24-28).

Conclusion

1. "When the Son of man cometh, shall he find faith on the earth" (Luke 18:8)?

2. The day of Christ's coming will be a day of great tragedy and triumph (2 Thessalonians 1:7-10). Which will it be for you?

~ 72 ~
There Shall Be a Resurrection

Introduction

1. Death is not the end of things! There shall be a resurrection (Acts 24:15).

2. The word resurrection means "a raising up…a rising from the dead."

3. There is a lot of speculation and misinformation about the resurrection. This is not new.

    a. The Sadducees denied it (Matthew 22:23; Acts 23:8).

    b. When some heard of it, they mocked (Acts 17:32).

    c. Paul was called into question of it (Acts 23:6; 24:21).

    d. Some among the Corinthians said, "there is no resurrection" (1 Corinthians 15:12).

    e. Hymenaeus and Philetus said it "is past already" (2 Timothy 2:18).

4. "There shall be a resurrection" is taught in both the Old and New Testaments.

Discussion

I. Glimpses of the resurrection in the Old Testament

    A. Genesis 5:24 is the first indication of a life beyond this one.

    B. Jesus appealed to Exodus 3:6 to affirm the resurrection (Matthew 22:31-32).

    C. Job asked, "If a man die, shall he live again?" (Job 14:14). He had confidence of a bodily resurrection at the latter day (Job 19:25-27).

D. David's statement in Psalm 16:8-11 was quoted by Peter in Acts 2:31 and applied to "the resurrection of Christ."

E. Statements in the Psalms (Psalm 17:15; 49:15; 73:24).

F. The statement in Isaiah 25:8 was quoted by Paul as he discussed the resurrection of the dead (1 Corinthians 15:54).

G. Notice Isaiah 26:19 and Hosea 13:14.

H. The resurrection is more fully revealed in the New Testament as Christ "brought life and immortality to light through the gospel" (2 Timothy 1:10).

II. New Testament teaching concerning the resurrection

A. The resurrection is certain.
 1. John 5:28-29
 2. Acts 24:15

B. The resurrection includes all.
 1. John 5:28-29
 2. None will be left!

C. The resurrection will take place by Christ's voice.
 1. John 11:43-44
 2. John 5:28-29

D. The resurrection reveals two groups of people.
 1. They that have done good and they that have done evil (John 5:29)
 2. The just and the unjust (Acts 24:15)

E. The resurrection declares two destinies.
 1. Life and damnation (John 5:29).
 2. This will be decided by what we have done in life.

F. The resurrection will be at the last day.
 1. John 6:39-40, 44, 54

            2. John 11:23-24
        G. The resurrection of all is assured by the resurrection of one.
            1. Acts 17:31
            2. 1 Corinthians 6:14
            3. 1 Corinthians 15:12-22
            4. 2 Corinthians 4:14
        H. The resurrection will be ushered in by Christ's coming.
            1. 1 Corinthians 15:23
            2. 1 Thessalonians 4:16
        I. The resurrection will bring forth a spiritual body.
            1. 1 Corinthians 15:35-50
            2. 2 Corinthians 4:16-5:4
            3. Philippians 3:20-21
            4. 1 John 3:2

Conclusion

1. In baptism, there is a death, burial and resurrection (Romans 6:3-5).
2. Because of our assurance of the resurrection, let us be faithful (1 Corinthians 15:58).

~ 73 ~
Standing Before the Judgment Seat of Christ

Introduction

1. Romans 14:10
2. The scriptures often speak of the judgment.
   a. Matthew 10:14-15; 11:20-24
   b. Matthew 25:31-46
   c. Acts 17:30-31
   d. Acts 24:25
   e. Hebrews 9:27
   f. Revelation 20:11-15
3. Six things about the judgment:

Discussion

I. The judgment is certain
   A. In picturing the judgment scene, 13 times Jesus used the word "shall" which indicates certainty (Matthew 25:31-34, 37, 40-41, 44-46).
   B. We shall all stand before the judgment (Romans 14:10).
   C. A day appointed (Acts 17:30-31)

II. The judgment will take place when Christ comes
   A. Matthew 25:31-32

- B. Matthew 16:27
- C. 2 Thessalonians 1:7-10
- D. 2 Peter 3:7, 10
- E. Since the time of His coming is unknown to us, we must always be ready!

III. The judgment will be administered by Christ
- A. Matthew 25:32
- B. Romans 14:10
- C. 2 Corinthians 5:10
- D. John 5:22
- E. Acts 10:42
- F. Acts 17:31
- G. Romans 2:16
- H. His judgment will be just (John 5:30). He is "the righteous judge" (2 Timothy 4:8). His word will be the standard (John 12:48).

IV. The judgment will be universal in scope
- A. Matthew 25:32
- B. Romans 14:10-12
- C. 2 Corinthians 5:10

V. The judgment will be individual in nature
- A. Matthew 25:34-45
- B. Romans 14:12
- C. 2 Corinthians 5:10
- D. We will be judged by our words (Matthew 12:36-37) and works (Matthew 16:27; Revelation 20:12).

VI. The judgment will determine our eternal destiny
- A. Matthew 25:46
- B. Where will you spend eternity?

Conclusion

1. Ecclesiastes 12:13-14
2. Should Christ appear this very hour and you stand before Him to be judged, will you hear Him say "enter" (Matthew 25:21) or "depart" (Matthew 7:23)?

~ 74 ~
Why All the Confusion Concerning the Holy Spirit?

Introduction

1. There is much confusion concerning the Holy Spirit.

2. It's not:

    a. Of God, "For God is not the author of confusion" (1 Corinthians 14:33).

    b. Due to a lack of information on the subject. The Bible has much to say about the Holy Spirit.

    c. The information we have can't be understood. It can (Ephesians 3:4)!

3. Why then all the confusion?

Discussion

I. A failure to know the scriptures

   A. Not knowing the Scriptures is the basic cause of religious error and confusion (Matthew 22:29).

   B. If folks would search the Scriptures (Acts 17:11) to find out what the Holy Spirit has revealed about Himself, instead of listening to the personal testimony of misguided men, they would not be so confused about the Holy Spirit! (1 Corinthians 2:5).

II. Not observing how the word "spirit" is used

   A. The first rule of grammar: No word is a part of speech until it first appears in context. Take the word "bear" for example (Genesis 4:13; 16:11; Exodus 20:16; 1 Samuel 17:34).

B. The word "spirit" occurs over 500 times in the Bible, and is used different ways depending on the context. For example:

1. Human spirit (James 2:26)
2. Attitude or disposition of a man (Galatians 6:1)
3. The Holy Spirit (John 7:39)

III. Losing sight of the fact that the Holy Spirit is a person

A. Personal pronouns require a person (John 16:13).

B. He demonstrates actions of a person: leads (Matthew 4:1), teaches and reminds (John 14:26), testifies (John 15:26), reproves (John 16:7-8), guides, speaks, hears and shows (John 16:13), forbids (Acts 16:6-7), bears witness (Romans 8:16), and searches (1 Corinthians 2:10).

C. He has things possessed by a person: knowledge (1 Corinthians 2:11) and will (1 Corinthians 12:11).

D. Things that can be done to Him show He is a person: He can be blasphemed (Matthew 12:31), lied to (Acts 5:3), resisted (Acts 7:51), grieved (Ephesians 4:30), and despised (Hebrews 10:29).

E. He is a divine person (Acts 5:3-4). He is as much a divine person as the Father and the Son are divine persons.

IV. Not realizing the Spirit works through the medium of the word

A. All action of the Holy Spirit in the conviction of sinners and edification of Christians is accomplished through the word of God.

B. Whatever influence one thinks the Holy Spirit exerts upon them, a passage can be produced which shows the Word of God accomplishes the same thing. This shows the Spirit works through the Word. Some examples: faith (Romans 10:17), begetting (James 1:18), quickening (Psalm 119:50), birth (1 Peter 1:23), salvation (James 1:21), cleansing (Psalm 119:9), purification (1 Peter 1:22), sanctification (John 17:17), dwelling (Colossians 3:16), leading (Psalm 119:105), comfort (1 Thessalonians 4:18), fruit (Colossians 1:5-6), growth

(1 Peter 2:2), strength (Acts 20:32).

C. If the Spirit works independent of the Word:
1. Does He work that way for everybody (Acts 10:34-35)?
2. Why are there no Christians where Bibles have not been sent and preachers have not gone?
3. Why are not all strong Christians? Do they have the Holy Spirit in differing degrees?
4. Why send for Peter (Acts 11:13-14)?

V. Diversity among those claiming direct influence of the Holy Spirit

A. Assemblies of God (Springfield, MO):
1. 3 persons in Godhead.
2. Water baptism NOT necessary.
3. Holy Spirit baptism AFTER salvation.

B. United Pentecostal Church (Hazelwood, MO):
1. 1 person in Godhead—Jesus only.
2. Water baptism necessary.
3. Holy Spirit baptism BEFORE salvation.

VI. Not recognizing the different manifestations of the Holy Spirit

A. Baptism of the Holy Spirit (Matthew 3:11; Acts 1:2-8; 2:4; 10-11).
B. Gift of the Holy Spirit (Acts 2:38-39).
C. Gifts of the Holy Spirit (1 Corinthians 12-14; Acts 8:18; 19:6; Hebrews 2:3-4).
D. Indwelling of the Holy Spirit (2 Timothy 1:14; Ephesians 5:18-19; Colossians 3:16).

Conclusion

1. All that can be known about the Holy Spirit is what the Holy Spirit has revealed about Himself in the Bible.
2. The Holy Spirit has revealed God's plan for saving man in the gospel (Ephesians 3:3-6; Romams 1:16). Come obeying it now as we sing!

~ 75 ~
Hold Fast the Pattern

Introduction

1. Prior to his departure, Paul issued the appeal, "Hold fast the pattern of sound words, which thou hast heard of me, in faith and love which is in Christ Jesus" (2 Timothy 1:13).
2. This is a call and cry that must be heard by every generation!

Discussion

I. We are familiar with patterns

   A. A rulebook: A game is played according to a set of rules. This set of rules serves as a restrictive pattern that ensures each game is played and umpired the same way, no matter where or when it is played.

   B. A blueprint: When a building is planned, someone draws up a blueprint. Everyone involved in the construction looks to the pattern so everything is put in place as planned. If the blueprint is ignored, the building would not be according to the pattern.

   C. A clothing pattern: Pieces laid out on fabric, cut along certain measurements and shapes, results in dresses of the same style.

II. God has used patterns

   A. The ark pattern (Genesis 6:14-16).

   B. The tabernacle pattern (Exodus 25:8-9, 40; Hebrews 8:5).

   C. The temple pattern (1 Chronicles 28:19, 11-12).

III. We must hold fast the pattern

  A. Whatever God says on a given subject constitutes the pattern for that issue.

  B. Some patterns to hold fast:

   1. The name pattern (Romans 16:16; Acts 11:26)

   2. The evangelism pattern (Acts 8:4; Philippians 4:15-16)

   3. The benevolence pattern (Acts 2, 4, 6; 11:27-30; 1 Timothy 5:16)

   4. The organization pattern (Ephesians 1:22-23; Philippians 1:1)

   5. The Lord's supper pattern (Matthew 26:26-29; Acts 20:7; 1 Corinthians 11:23-34)

   6. The music pattern (Ephesians 5:19; Colossians 3:16)

   7. The conversion pattern (Acts 2-19; 1 Timothy 1:16)

   8. The return and restoration pattern (Acts 8:20-22)

Conclusion

1. God's pattern is perfect (James 1:25). It is not to be added to or subtracted from (Deuteronomy 4:2; Revelation 22:18-19). It contains all things (2 Peter 1:3).

2. Binding in every church (1 Corinthians 4:17; 7:17). Results in unity (Philippians 3:16).

~ 76 ~
Ensamples Written for Our Admonition

Introduction

1. 1 Corinthians 10:1-13

2. In chapters 8-10, Paul is discussing a Christian's liberty; things within the realm of that which is lawful (10:23). He appeals to the example of Israel to warn the strong to be careful lest they fall into sin.

Discussion

I. All delivered from Egypt

   A. Verses 1-5

   B. Notice the five "all's" (how Israel was blessed by God):

   1. All were under the cloud (v. 1). "And the Lord went before them by day in a pillar of a cloud, to lead them the way… He took not away the pillar of the cloud by day…from before the people" (Exodus 13:21-22).

   2. All passed through the sea (v. 1). "And Moses stretched out his hand over the sea; and the Lord caused the sea to go back by a strong east wind all that night, and made the sea dry land, and the waters were divided. And the children of Israel went into the midst of the sea upon the dry ground" (Exodus 14:21-22; Hebrews 11:29).

   3. All were baptized unto Moses (v. 2). By passing through the sea as they did, they were completely covered by the sea and the cloud. Thus, they were "baptized" unto Moses.

Sermons for the Seed Sower

      4. All ate the same spiritual meat (v. 3): bread from heaven called "manna" (Exodus 16:1-36).

      5. All drank the same spiritual drink (v. 4). God provided water for them out of a rock (Exodus 17:1-7).

II. Many of them overthrown in the wilderness

   A. But with many of them God was not well pleased, for they were overthrown in the wilderness (v. 5).

   B. Other translations: "most of them"

III. Things which contributed to their fall

   A. Lust (v. 6)

      1. Numbers 11:4-6

      2. Psalm 106:10-14

      3. We must guard against such (James 1:14-15; 2 Peter 1:4; 1 John 2:16-17).

   B. Idolatry (v. 7)

      1. Committed when Israel fashioned the golden calf (Exodus 32:6, 19, 25)

      2. The Bible often warns of such (1 Corinthians 6:9; 10:14; Galatians 5:20; Colossians 3:5).

   C. Fornication (v. 8)

      1. This takes us back to the scene in Numbers 25:1-9.

      2. We must flee such (1 Corinthians 6:13, 18; 7:2; Ephesians 5:3; 1 Thessalonians 4:3).

   D. Tempting Christ (v. 9)

      1. Numbers 21:5-6

      2. The Corinthians did the same when they provoked the Lord to jealousy by attending feasts in the idol's temple (1 Corinthians 10:22).

   E. Murmuring (v. 10)

      1. God never has tolerated complaining (Numbers 14:1-37).

      2. John 6:43

3. Philippians 2:14

Conclusion

1. These things were written for our admonition (vv. 11-13)!
2. We must take heed (Hebrews 3:12-4:1)!

~ 77 ~
Why So Many Churches?

Introduction

1. Not a question asked in the first century—only one church existed.
2. A question that is asked today—many different churches in existence. Why?

Discussion

I. It's not because

   A. God planned many—planned one (Ephesians 3:10-11)

   B. Christ built many—built one (Matthew 16:18)

   C. Christ is Head over many—Head over one (Ephesians 1:21-23; Colossians 1:18)

   D. Christ is Saviour of many—Saviour of one (Ephesians 5:23)

   E. Christ purchased many—purchased one (Acts 20:28)

II. It's because

   A. There has been a falling away.

      1. The Lord and the apostles predicted apostasy (Matthew 7:15-16; Acts 20:29-31; 2 Thessalonians 2:3, 7; 1 Timothy 4:1-3).

      2. In the second century, there began to be a distinction made between an elder and a bishop. There is no such distinction in the Bible (Acts 20:17, 28; Titus 1:5-9; 1 Peter 5:1-2).

      3. A change in the form of government from a plurality

of bishops over one church (Philippians 1:1) to a single bishop of a plurality of churches.

    4. This gave rise to Roman Catholicism. There were changes in other areas as well: original sin, infant baptism, auricular confession, sale of indulgences, etc.

  B. Attempts to reform the Roman Catholic Church

    1. There were various reformers like Martin Luther who protested against the Roman Catholic Church.

    2. Thus began the Period of the Reformation. This spawned a number of distinct denominations that did not exist prior to the sixteenth century (Lutheran Church, Presbyterian, Episcopalian, Baptist, Methodist, etc.).

    3. Along came human creeds—different faiths.

  C. Divisions within the church

    1. Plea for unity (Psalm 133; John 17; 1 Corinthians 1:10)

    2. 1849—controversy over Missionary Society

    3. 1859—mechanical instruments of music

    4. 1906—U.S. Census recognized Christian Church as a separate religious body from the church of Christ

    5. 1950s-60s—issue of support of human institutions from the church treasury, social gospel concept

Conclusion

1. Our plea is to return to the original doctrine of Christ and restore the original church of Christ.

2. Come now as we sing!

~ 78 ~
The Classic Parable Collection

Introduction

1. Nowhere else is there so rich a group of parables as the classic parable collection found in Matthew 13.

2. Jesus went out of the house and sat by the seaside. Great multitudes were gathered together unto Him, so that He went into a ship. The whole multitude stood on the shore. Using a ship as His pulpit, Jesus spake many things in parables (Matthew 13:1-3).

Discussion

I. What are parables?

   A. In the New Testament, the word "parable" means "to cast alongside, a placing beside; a comparison."

   B. Parables are comparisons of earthly things with heavenly things; simple stories placed beside heavenly truths.

   C. Thus, a parable is an earthly story with a heavenly meaning.

II. The purpose of parables

   A. To reveal: Through parables, hidden truths would be revealed to those with seeing eyes and hearing ears (Matthew 13:10-17).

   B. To conceal: Through parables, truths would be withheld from those with waxed-gross hearts, dull-of-hearing ears, and closed eyes (Matthew 13:10-17). In them is fulfilled the prophecy of Isaiah (Isaiah 6:9-10).

C. To fulfill: Jesus' speaking in parables fulfilled prophecy (Matthew 13:34-35; Psalm 78:1-2).

III. Seven consecutive parables

　A. Parable of the sower (Matthew 13:3-9, 18-23)—take heed how ye hear!

　　1. The seed—the word of the kingdom (v. 19)

　　2. The soils—different kinds of hearts:

　　　a. Wayside (v. 4): He that hears the word and does not understand it; the devil comes and catches away that which was sown (v. 19).

　　　b. Stony (vv. 5-6): He that hears and receives the word with joy but has no root. When tribulation and persecution come because of the word, he is offended (vv. 20-21).

　　　c. Thorny (v. 7): He that hears the word and the care of this world and the deceitfulness of riches choke the word and he becomes unfruitful (v. 22).

　　　d. Good ground (v. 8): He that hears and understands the word and brings forth fruit, some an hundredfold, some sixty, some thirty (v. 23).

　B. Parable of the tares (Matthew 13:24-30, 36-43). This begins a series of parables that start with the phrase, "The kingdom of heaven is like…" Answers questions about good and evil: What are the origins of each? Why do good people have to live along side wicked people? Will good ever triumph over evil?

　　1. The sowers:

　　　a. Man sowed good seed in his field (v. 24)—the Son of man (v. 37)

　　　b. Enemy came and sowed tares (v. 25)—the devil (v. 39)

　　2. The wheat and tares:

　　　a. The good seed, wheat (vv. 24-25)—the children of the kingdom (v. 38)

　　　b. Tares, a kind of darnel resembling wheat except that

the grains are black (vv. 25-26)—the children of the wicked one (v. 38)
3. The field (v. 24)—the world (v. 38)
4. The harvest and the reapers (v. 30)—the end of the world when the Son of man sends forth his angels, and they gather out of his kingdom all things that offend and them which do iniquity and they are cast into a furnace of fire (vv. 39-42)

C. Parable of the mustard seed (Matthew 13:31-32)—growth of the kingdom
1. The least of all seeds, when planted, grows to the greatest among herbs and becomes a tree so that the birds come and lodge in the branches.
2. From a man crying in the wilderness to a carpenter's son from Nazareth (John 1:46), the kingdom of God began to be preached (Matthew 3:1-2; 4:17). Jesus taught His disciples and the disciples taught the nations (Matthew 28:19; Acts 8:4).
3. This is as prophesied (Daniel 2:35).

D. Parable of the leaven (Matthew 13:33)—growth of the kingdom
1. Leaven is used in the Scriptures for either good or bad; it represents a strong and pervasive influence (Matthew 16:6; 1 Corinthians 5:6; Galatians 5:9).
2. Represents the silent, permeating influence of the kingdom and the gospel among men.

E. Parable of the treasure hid in a field (Matthew 13:34)—value of the kingdom
1. The man found the treasure without seeking for it.
2. He recognized its value, sold all that he had and bought the field.

F. Parable of the pearl of great price (Matthew 13:45-46)—value of the kingdom.
1. The man was seeking goodly pearls, found one pearl of great price.

2. He sold all that he had and bought it.

G. Parable of the net cast into the sea (Matthew 13:47-50)—final separation of the good from the bad.

1. The kingdom is like a net cast into the sea and gathers of every kind. It is drawn to shore; the good gathered into vessels and the bad cast away.

2. This pictures the judgment when the wicked are separated from the just.

Conclusion

1. Let's take heed how we hear. Be that good soil, that when the seed is planted in our heart we receive it and bring forth fruit. Recognize there is good and evil in this world and that good will ultimately triumph over evil. Let the kingdom grow in our hearts, recognize the value of the kingdom, and pay every price necessary to enter it so that when the net is drawn to shore, we will be judged good enough to keep.

2. We invite you to obey the gospel now as we stand and sing!

~ 79 ~
Tell Your Children

Introduction

1. Joel 1:3

2. Every generation has the responsibility of telling the next generation the things of the Lord (Deuteronomy 4:9; 6:7-9; 11:18-21), lest there arise a generation that does not know the Lord! (Judges 2:10).

3. Some things to tell your children:

Discussion

I. There is a God

   A. Genesis 1:1

   B. Psalm 14:1

   C. That God made them (Genesis 1:26-27; 2:7) and it is in Him that they have their being (Acts 17:28).

   D. About God's love for them (John 3:16; Romans 5:8).

   E. That they are accountable to God (Ecclesiastes 12:13-14; Romans 14:12).

II. That the Bible is the word of God

   A. 2 Timothy 3:16-17

   B. 2 Peter 1:20-21

   C. That it is not just a good book among many. It is the book of books!

D. The fact that it contains all things they need spiritually (2 Peter 1:3).

III. About God's marriage law

   A. That marriage originated with God (Genesis 2:18-24)

   B. That it involves one man and one woman for one lifetime (Matthew 19:4-6; Romans 7:2-3)

   C. That the Lord hates divorce (Malachi 2:16) and that it was not so from the beginning (Matthew 19:8)

IV. About Jesus

   A. That He is the Son of God, the Saviour, the King of kings, etc.

   B. About His life, His death on the cross, His burial, His resurrection, His appearances, His ascension, and the fact that He is coming again

V. About the New Testament church

   A. The fact that there is one church (Ephesians 4:4; Colossians 1:24).

   B. About its origin, name, work, worship, organization, and destiny

VI. About the judgment to come

   A. Acts 24:25

   B. How to prepare for it: by HBRCBF.

Conclusion

1. If we don't tell our children, they may never know.

2. Someone will tell them something. Who will it be and what will they be told?

~ 80 ~
Consequences of Keeping the Law of Moses

Introduction

1. Since the Old Testament law of Moses has served its purpose and been done away with, there are some consequences of keeping the law of Moses today.

2. If one keeps the law of Moses today, these are the results:

Discussion

I. Makes justification impossible

   A. Justification is the process by which sinful man is declared or made righteous in the sight of God.

   B. This occurs not by the works of the law, but by the faith of Christ.

      1. Galatians 2:16

      2. Galatians 3:11

   C. One simply cannot keep the law of Moses and be justified!

II. Causes some things to be in vain

   A. The word "vain" suggests "useless, having no meaning."

   B. Three examples:

      1. Christ died in vain (Galatians 2:21).

      2. Brethren suffered in vain (Galatians 3:4).

      3. Paul laboured in vain (Galatians 4:11).

III. Puts one under a curse
   A. Galatians 3:10, 13-14
   B. Why be under a curse, when you can be blessed?
IV. Reduces one to servant status
   A. Paul uses the illustration of an heir as a child (under the age of legal responsibility) versus a son (legally considered an adult) (Galatians 4:1-7).
   B. Why revert back to being a child when you are a son and possess the Father's blessings?
V. Puts one in bondage
   A. The law of Moses was "a yoke…which neither our fathers nor we were able to bear" (Acts 15:10).
   B. Galatians 5:1
   C. Why be in bondage when Christ has made us free?
VI. Makes Christ unprofitable
   A. Galatians 5:2
   B. Christ is of no help or benefit to the individual that is circumcised as a condition for receiving salvation.
VII. Obligates one to do the whole law
   A. Galatians 5:3
   B. If we keep one command of the law, we are obligated to keep every other command of the law. This would demand that we go to Jerusalem to worship, offer animal sacrifices, keep the dietary regulations, and every other requirement of the law.
VIII. Makes Christ of none effect
   A. Galatians 5:4
   B. To keep the law is to be estranged from Christ, and to be estranged from Christ is to be cut off from all spiritual blessings (Ephesians 1:3)!
IX. Causes one to fall from grace
   A. Galatians 5:4

B. This deals a crushing blow to the doctrine of the perseverance of the saints, "once in grace, always in grace."

C. One who is seeking to be justified by the law of Moses has fallen from grace.

D. You do not want to fall from grace, for "by grace ye are saved" (Ephesians 2:5).

X. Makes the apostles false teachers

A. The apostles were guided into all truth (John 16:13). They taught that we are "dead to the law" (Romans 7:4) and "delivered from the law" (Romans 7:6). They revealed that the Old Testament was "done away" (2 Corinthians 3:7, 11, 14) and "abolished" (2 Corinthians 3:13; Ephesians 2:15).

B. If the law is still in effect and is to be kept, then the apostles were wrong. If the apostles are right, then those who keep the law and teach men to do so must be wrong. Which is it?

XI. Disqualifies Christ from the priesthood

A. According to the law, one had to be of the tribe of Levi to be a priest (Numbers 3:5-10).

B. Hebrews 7:14; 8:4

C. Yet, the Lord is not only a priest, He is "a great high priest" (Hebrews 4:14).

D. Only way this is possible is the law must have changed (Hebrews 7:12).

XII. Shows disrespect for the authority of Christ

A. Christ has "all authority in heaven and in earth" (Matthew 28:18).

B. The transfiguration scene (Matthew 17:1-5)

C. God has spoken unto us in these last days by His Son (Hebrews 1:1-2).

D. Christ is the Prophet raised up like unto Moses, whom we are to hear in all things (Acts 3:22-23).

E. We are to do all in His name or by His authority (Colossians 3:17).

Conclusion

1. The law of Moses is no longer a standard of judgment (Colossians 2:14-17).

2. In the judgment to come, we will be judged by the word of Christ (John 12:48). Being "under the law to Christ" (1 Corinthians 9:21), let us "fulfil the law of Christ" (Galatians 6:2).

~ 81 ~
What Is the Church of Christ?

Introduction

1. Many have no idea what the church of Christ is.
2. The church of Christ is set forth on the pages of the word of God in various figures to help us understand what the church is. Thus, we study.

Discussion

I. The church of Christ is the body of Christ

   A. The church is the body and the body is the church (Ephesians 1:22-23; Colossians 1:24).

   B. There is one body (Ephesians 4:4).

   C. Christ is the Head (Colossians 1:18; Ephesians 1:22-23; 4:15; 5:23).

   D. Notice Paul's teaching concerning the body (1 Corinthians 12:12-27).

   E. As the body of Christ, the church is the circle of the called (Colossians 3:15), the realm of the reconciled (Ephesians 2:16) and the sphere of the saved (Ephesians 5:23).

   F. Entrance into the body is by baptism (1 Corinthians 12:13; Acts 2:41, 47).

II. The church of Christ is the bride of Christ

   A. 2 Corinthians 11:2

   B. Romans 7:4

C. This relationship requires that the church be subject unto Christ (Ephesians 5:22-25).

   D. As the bride of Christ, the church wears the name of Christ (Romans 16:16; Acts 11:26).

   E. To suggest there is more than one church is to accuse Christ of being a polygamist!

III. The church of Christ is the flock of God

   A. John 10:1

   B. A sheepfold is an enclosure, fold or pen, much like today's barn. Hence, one must be in the proper enclosure to be part of the flock of God.

   C. Christ is the good shepherd (John 10:11, 14), the great shepherd (Hebrews 13:20), and the chief shepherd (1 Peter 5:4).

   D. The disciples of Christ are His sheep (Acts 20:28; 1 Peter 5:2).

   E. Straying sheep must be found and brought home (Luke 15:4-7).

IV. The church of Christ is the house of God

   A. The church of Christ is God's spiritual family or household (Ephesians 2:19; 3:15; 1 Timothy 3:15; 1 Peter 2:5).

   B. Several things are implied by the household figure:

      1. A father (Ephesians 4:6)

      2. Children (Galatians 3:26-29)

      3. An inheritance (Romans 8:14-17; 1 Peter 1:3-4)

V. The church of Christ is the kingdom of God

   A. The Scriptures often use the terms "church" and "kingdom" interchangeably (Matthew 16:18-19; Colossians 1:13, 22, 24; Hebrews 12:23, 28).

   B. The kingdom figure presents the aspect of government. The kingdom of God is an absolute monarchy with Christ as King (1 Timothy 6:15; Revelation 17:14; 19:16).

   C. The kingdom is spiritual in nature (John 18:36; Romans 14:17).

- D. Kingdom citizenship is by a spiritual new birth (John 3:3-7; 1 Corinthians 4:15; James 1:18; 1 Peter 1:23).
- E. The ultimate destiny of the kingdom is to be delivered up to God (1 Corinthians 15:24).

VI. The church of Christ is the temple of God

- A. This suggests a place where God meets with His people as they worship Him.
- B. The temple built by Solomon became a place of worship for Jews in the Old Testament (2 Chronicles 7:12-16).
- C. The church of Christ is God's New Testament temple (1 Corinthians 3:16-17; Ephesians 2:19-22). Christians are God's building (1 Corinthians 3:9).

VII. The church of Christ is the vineyard of the Lord

- A. The Lord likened His church to a vineyard (Matthew 20:1-16).
- B. As the vineyard of the Lord, the church is a workplace.
    1. A father told his sons, "Go work to day in my vineyard" (Matthew 21:28-30).
    2. "A vineyard calls for harder and more regular labor than any other form of agriculture" (*Zondervan Pictorial Encyclopedia*, p. 882).
- C. Every Christian is a laborer in the Lord's vineyard (1 Corinthians 15:58).

Conclusion

1. Now that you know what the church of Christ is, as defined and described on the pages of God's word, you are in better position to identify it.

2. Will you become a member of the body, married to Christ, a sheep in the flock, a child of God, a kingdom citizen, to worship in His temple and labor in His vineyard?

~ 82 ~
When the Day of Pentecost Was Come

Introduction

1. Acts 2:1
2. The day of Pentecost, called the feast of weeks in the Old Testament, was an annual feast day of the Jews that came 50 days after the Passover upon which the first fruits were offered unto the Lord (Leviticus 23:15-16; Deuteronomy 16:10, 16).
3. This study brings to our attention some things which came when the day of Pentecost was come, as recorded in Acts 2.

Discussion

I. The promise of the Father came

   A. The apostles were instructed to tarry in Jerusalem for the promise of the Father (Luke 24:49).

   B. The promise of the Father was baptism with the Holy Spirit (Acts 1:4-5). This promise was limited as to:

   1. Persons—the apostles (Acts 1:2)
   2. Place—Jerusalem (Acts 1:4)
   3. Period—Not many days hence (Acts 1:5)
   4. Purpose—to empower apostles as witnesses unto Christ (Acts 1:8)

   C. This promise came when the day of Pentecost was come, as Acts 2:4 shows.

II. Tongue speaking came

A. In the giving of the Great Commission, one of the signs to follow them that believe was, "they shall speak with new tongues" (Mark 16:17). These signs served to confirm the word (Mark 16:20).

B. The supernatural ability to speak with new tongues, languages one did not know and had not studied, came when the day of Pentecost was come (Acts 2:4-11).

C. This miraculous ability ceased when divine revelation was complete (1 Corinthians 13:8-13).

III. Fulfillment of prophecy came

A. When men confused speaking with new tongues for being full of new wine, Peter said, "this is that which was spoken by the prophet Joel," and quoted Joel 2:28-32 as having its fulfillment when the day of Pentecost was come (Acts 2:13-21).

B. Fulfilled prophecy is one of the greatest evidences that the Bible did not originate with man, but with God (2 Peter 1:20-21).

IV. The last days came

A. There's a lot of confusion about the last days.

B. Acts 2:16-17 shows that the last days came when the day of Pentecost was come.

C. Some things the Bible says about the last days:

1. Lord's house to be established (Isaiah 2:2)

2. Perilous times to come (2 Timothy 3:1)

3. God hath spoken by His Son (Hebrews 1:1-2)

4. Scoffers to come (2 Peter 3:3)

V. Preaching as prescribed in the great commission came

A. The Lord commissioned His apostles to go preach (Matthew 28:18-20; Mark 16:15-16; Luke 24:46-49).

B. This was first executed when the day of Pentecost was come. Acts 2:22-36 records Peter's sermon.

1. He preached the death, burial, resurrection, and exaltation of Christ.

      2. Acts 2:37-38, 41 shows the results of such preaching.

VI. The house/kingdom/church came

   A. Old Testament prophets looked forward to the establishment of the church.

      1. House (Isaiah 2:2-3; 1 Timothy 3:15)

      2. Kingdom (Daniel 2:44; Matthew 16:18)

   B. Prior to Acts 2, always spoken of as being in the future.

      1. At hand (Matthew 4:17)

      2. To come (Matthew 6:10)

      3. Will build (Matthew 16:18)

      4. Disciples to see it come (Mark 9:1)

   C. When the day of Pentecost was come, the first time the church is spoken of as being in existence (Acts 2:47).

      1. Came as a result of the word being preached, folks hearing it, believing it and obeying it!

      2. You can become a member the same way!

Conclusion

1. Pentecost, what a day! It's the beginning (Luke 24:49; Acts 11:15).

2. There's no better time for you to be added to the church than today (2 Corinthians 6:2)!

~ 83 ~
Six Things All Men Have

Introduction

1. There may be some things you have that I don't. Yet, there are some things we have in common.

2. Let me point out six things all men have.

Discussion

I. All men have a soul

    A. Some try to strip man of his soul by denying that man has a soul.

    B. The Bible affirms the soul of man.

        1. Genesis 2:7

        2. Job 32:8

        3. Ecclesiastes 12:7

        4. Zechariah 12:1

        5. Matthew 10:28; 16:26

        6. James 2:26

II. All men have free will

    A. The Calvinist's concept of predestination that God chose the individual to be saved or lost without involving his choice robs man of his freewill.

    B. The Bible teaches we are creatures possessing the power and privilege of choice.

1. Genesis 2:16-17; 3:4
2. Joshua 24:15
3. Hebrews 11:25
4. Revelation 22:17

III. All men have sin in their life

   A. Romans 3:23

   B. Galatians 3:22

   C. We are not made sinners by birth, but become sinners by transgression (1 John 3:4).

   1. Deuteronomy 24:16
   2. Ezekiel 18:20

   D. We are influenced to sin the same way Eve was—through lust (2 Corinthians 11:3; 2 Peter 1:4; James 1:13-15; 1 John 2:16).

IV. All men have accountability

   A. Some seem to think they are not answerable or accountable to anyone.

   B. God made us accountable (Psalm 144:3).

   C. The day of judgment will be a day of accountability (Romans 14:12; Matthew 12:36; 2 Corinthians 5:10; 1 Peter 4:5).

V. All men have the same amount of time

   A. How many hours are there in your day?

   B. Time is short (Psalm 89:47; Job 14:1-2; James 4:14).

   C. We must redeem the time and awake to our responsibilities before God (Ephesians 5:16; Romans 13:11).

VI. All men have an appointment with death

   A. Hebrews 9:27

   B. Job 16:22; 30:23

   C. Thus, we must make arrangements for it by obeying the gospel and being faithful and steadfast so that when the occasion comes to us we will be ready for it!

Conclusion

1. Will you exercise your freewill today, while you have time and opportunity, in choosing to obey the gospel that you may rid your soul of sin, that when death comes and you stand to give account before God, you may hear the words, "Well done good and faithful servant: enter thou into the joy of thy lord" (Matthew 25:21)?

2. Come now!

~ 84 ~
Preaching What We Practice

Introduction

1. We often emphasize practicing what we preach and rightly so (Romans 2:21-23).
2. This lesson is about preaching what we practice. Suppose I preached what we practice. What would I preach?

Discussion

I. Concerning attendance

    A. Would I preach that it is okay to miss for every ache and pain?

    B. Would I preach that it's not necessary to attend all the services?

    C. Would I preach attend only if there's no conflict or nothing else to do?

    D. Would I preach put first things first (Matthew 6:33)?

    E. Would I preach not forsaking the assembling (Hebrews 10:25)?

    F. What would I preach if I preached what we practice concerning attendance?

II. Concerning hospitality

    A. Would I preach anything at all? Is it practiced at all?

    B. Would I preach that you ought to do it grudgingly?

    C. Would I preach that you only do it in return for what others do?

- D. Would I preach given to hospitality (Romans 12:13)?
- E. Would I preach be not forgetful to entertain (Hebrews 13:2)?
- F. Would I preach use hospitality one to another without grudging (1 Peter 4:9)?
- G. What would I preach if I preached what we practice when it comes to hospitality?

III. Concerning giving
- A. Would I preach that Jesus gave it all and we have nothing to give?
- B. Would I preach just give the Lord the leftovers?
- C. Would I preach that a man ought to rob God (Malachi 3:8)?
- D. Would I preach that it really doesn't matter how or what you give?
- E. Would I preach give weekly as prospered by the Lord (1 Corinthians 16:1-2)?
- F. Would I preach give bountifully, not grudgingly, but cheerfully (2 Corinthians 9:6-7)?
- G. Would I preach give sacrificially (2 Samuel 24:24; Mark 12:41-44)?
- H. What would I preach if I preached what we practice in regard to our giving?

IV. Concerning modesty
- A. Would I preach wear what you want when you want, it really doesn't matter?
- B. Would I preach wear the latest fashions out of Hollywood?
- C. Would I preach the shame of nakedness (Genesis 3:7-10; Isaiah 47:2-3)?
- D. Would I preach 1 Timothy 2:9-10?
- E. What would I preach if I preached what we practice concerning modesty?

V. Concerning care and concern for others
   A. Would I preach that we ought to be selfish, uninterested in affairs of others?
   B. Would I preach treat others as they treat us?
   C. Would I preach love others as self (Matthew 22:39; 7:12)?
   D. Would I preach look on the things of others (Philippians 2:4)?
   E. Would I preach teach others (2 Timothy 2:2)?
   F. Would I preach have the same care, suffer and rejoice (1 Corinthians 12:25-26)?
   G. What would I preach if I preached what we practice when it comes to showing care and concern for others?

VI. Concerning speech
   A. Would I preach that it doesn't matter what you say or how you say it?
   B. Would I preach okay to tell a little white lie?
   C. Would I preach that gossip and talebearing are acceptable?
   D. Would I preach that it is okay to take the Lord's name in vain?
   E. Would I preach against the sins of the tongue (Psalm 39:1)?
   F. Would I preach let thy words be few (Ecclesiastes 5:2)?
   G. Would I preach sound speech, that cannot be condemned (Titus 2:8)?
   H. What would I preach if I preached what we practice concerning speech?

Conclusion

1. What are we practicing?
2. We need to examine ourselves and make sure our practice is in line with what the Bible teaches (2 Corinthians 13:5).

~ 85 ~
A Ribband of Blue

Introduction

1. Numbers 15:37-41

2. The ribband of blue was the ribband of remembrance. The ribband is woven throughout the Scriptures as the Lord's people are to be a remembering people (Deuteronomy 5:15; 7:18; 8:2, 18; 9:7; 15:15; 16:3, 12; 24:9, 18, 22; 25:17; 32:7).

Discussion

I. Remember how short time is

    A. Psalm 89:47

    B. As a flower (Job 14:1-2)

    C. As a shadow (1 Chronicles 29:15)

    D. As a wind (Psalm 78:39)

    E. As a post (Job 9:25)

    F. As the swift ships (Job 9:26)

    G. As the eagle (Job 9:26)

    H. As a tale that is told (Psalm 90:9)

    I. As a weaver's shuttle (Job 7:6)

    J. As a vapour (James 4:14)

II. Remember thy creator

    A. Ecclesiastes 12:1

    B. Man has a Creator (Psalm 100:3; Genesis 1:26-27; 2:7).

    C. We are to be mindful of our responsibilities to God in our youth.

III. Remember Lot's wife

    A. Luke 17:32

    B. This takes us back to the scene in Genesis 19:17-26.

    C. Lot's wife stands as an enduring monument to the fact that God means what He says and that man must do as God says!

IV. Remember the words of the Lord

    A. John 15:20

    B. John 16:4

    C. Acts 20:35

    D. The words of the apostles are the words of the Lord (Jude 17; 1 Corinthians 14:37).

V. Remember them in bonds

    A. Hebrews 13:3

    B. As bound with them is an expression of compassion (Hebrews 10:34).

    C. Remember in prayer (Ephesians 6:18-20).

    D. Remembrance of them in bonds may give us boldness (Philippians 1:14).

VI. Remember from whence thou art fallen

    A. Revelation 2:5

    B. The Bible warns us about falling (1 Corinthians 10:12; Galatians 5:4).

    C. The prodigal son remembered (Luke 15:17). The first step in returning is remembering! Some never return because they never remember. We need to help them remember!

Conclusion

1. A good memory is important to us (1 Corinthians 15:1-2).

2. 1 Timothy 4:6

3. 2 Peter 1:12-15

~ 86 ~
Is the Seed Yet in the Barn?

Introduction

1. Haggai 2:19

2. I'm making spiritual application of this question today.

    a. The Lord's word is set forth as seed and the hearts of men and women are represented by soil (Luke 8:5-15).

    b. Every farmer knows that if the seed is left in the barn, there won't be a crop. It's our spiritual task to get the seed out of the barn and put it in the soil.

    c. The Psalmist said, "He that goeth forth and weepeth, bearing precious seed, shall doubtless come again with rejoicing, bringing his sheaves with him" (Psalm 126:6).

    d. Look at some examples of folks who got the seed out of the barn and put it in the soil.

Discussion

I. Anna got the seed out of the barn

    A. Luke 2:38

    B. When she spake of him to all them that looked for redemption in Jerusalem.

II. Andrew got the seed out of the barn

    A. John 1:40-42

    B. When he found his brother and brought him to Jesus.

III. Philip got the seed out of the barn
   A. John 1:45-51
   B. When he found Nathanael and he came to Jesus
IV. A woman of Samaria got the seed out of the barn
   A. John 4:25-30, 39
   B. When she went into the city and said, "Come"
V. Peter got the seed out of the barn
   A. Acts 2
   B. When he preached Jesus of Nazareth on Pentecost. The seed was mixed with good soil as they that gladly received his word were baptized (v. 41).
VI. Philip got the seed out of the barn
   A. Acts 8
   B. When he went to Samaria and preached Christ unto them (vv. 5-25).
   C. When he preached Jesus to the Ethiopian treasurer (vv. 26-39).

Conclusion

1. May these examples inspire us to get the seed out of the barn today.
2. And may the Lord give the increase (1 Corinthians 3:6).

~ 87 ~
And They All Began to Make Excuse

Introduction

1. Luke 14:16-24

2. In trying to get folks to obey the gospel, there are a number of excuses offered for not becoming a member of the church.

Discussion

I. I've been too bad

    A. God can make the best of the worst.

    B. Consider the Corinthians (1 Corinthians 6:9-11).

    C. Remember who Paul was (1 Timothy 1:13, 15).

II. My parents made me go when I was young

    A. Your parents made you do lots of things you may not have wanted to do that were in your best interest.

    B. Did they make you go to the doctor and take your medicine?

    C. Did they make you take a bath?

    D. Did they make you go to school?

III. There are too many hypocrites in the church

    A. No doubt there are some who are just playacting.

    B. They have their reward (Matthew 23).

    C. Don't let a hypocrite stand between you and God!

IV. I'm waiting until the time is right
   A. Psalm 39:7
   B. Proverbs 27:1
   C. Acts 22:16
   D. Hebrews 10:37
   E. The teaching of the Lord calls on us to be ready at all times (Matthew 24:48-51).
   F. Now is the right time (2 Corinthians 6:2).
V. I'm too old
   A. Ecclesiastes 12
   B. Some don't let age keep them from doing things they really want to do.
VI. I don't know enough yet
   A. Knowledge is important (John 6:44-45; 8:32).
   B. You never get to the point where you know it all.
   C. What is there that you don't know that you feel like you need to know before you become a Christian?

Conclusion
1. You're invited.
2. Come now, leaving all excuses behind.

~ 88 ~
When I Left the World

Introduction

1. John 15:18-19

2. We are called or chosen out of the world by the gospel (Ephesians 1:3; 2 Thessalonians 2:14). I made a decision early in life to answer the call of the gospel and leave the world.

3. Here are some things I left when I left the world:

Discussion

I. Evil works for good
   A. John 7:7
   B. John 3:19
   C. Galatians 1:4; Titus 2:14
   D. Romans 12:9
   E. 1 Thessalonians 5:22
   F. 3 John 11

II. Darkness for light
   A. John 8:12
   B. John 12:46
   C. Acts 26:18
   D. Romans 13:12
   E. 1 Peter 2:9

III. Death for life
   A. Mark 10:30
   B. John 5:24
IV. Tribulation for peace
   A. John 16:33
   B. Ephesians 2:14
   C. Romans 2:9-10
V. Enmity for friendship
   A. James 4:4
   B. Romans 8:7
   C. Romans 5:9; Colossians 1:21
   D. John 15:14
VI. The temporal for the eternal
   A. 1 John 2:17
   B. 2 Corinthians 4:16-18
   C. Hebrews 11:10, 13-16; 13:14
VII. Corruption for cleanness
   A. 2 Peter 1:4
   B. 2 Peter 2:18, 20
   C. 1 John 1:7, 9

Conclusion

1. The call of the gospel continues to ring this day. Will you leave the world?
2. If you've left the Lord and gone back into the world, realize what you have left!

~ 89 ~
They Continued Stedfastly

Introduction

1. Acts 2:42

2. We have in one sentence the most comprehensive statement capturing the devotion and faithfulness of the first converts.

Discussion

I. They (Who are they?)

   A. Jews, devout men, out of every nation under heaven dwelling at Jerusalem (Acts 2:5), present for "the day of Pentecost (Acts 2:1), an annual feast day of the Jews, which came 50 days after Passover, upon which they presented "the firstfruits unto the Lord" (Leviticus 23:15-17).

   B. Those among the multitude who came together after the apostles were all filled with the Holy Ghost and heard them speak in their languages the wonderful works of God (Acts 2:2-4, 6-11).

   C. Those who heard the words preached by Peter and "…were pricked in their heart and said…, Men and brethren, what shall we do?" (Acts 2:37).

   D. Those who were told, "Repent, and be baptized every one of you in the name of Jesus Christ for the remission of sins" (Acts 2:38).

   E. Those who were exhorted with many other words to save themselves (Acts 2:40).

   F. They that gladly received the word, were baptized, about 3,000 souls (Acts 2:41).

II. Continued (What did they do?)
   A. John 8:31
   B. Acts 13:43
   C. Acts 14:21-22
   D. Colossians 1:22-23
   E. 2 Timothy 3:14
   F. James 1:25

III. Stedfastly (How did they continue?)
   A. They persevered. They did not waver. They were constantly diligent.
   B. 1 Corinthians 15:58
   C. Hebrews 3:14
   D. 1 Peter 5:8-9
   E. Colossians 2:5
   F. 2 Peter 3:17

IV. In (What did they continue stedfastly in?)
   A. The apostles' doctrine
      1. The apostles were men chosen and sent out by the Lord to teach and preach the gospel (Matthew 28:19-20; Mark 16:15-16).
      2. The apostles' doctrine is their teaching. It is backed by the authority of Christ (Matthew 10:40; 1 Corinthians 14:37; Galatians 1:11-12). They were given the Holy Spirit to guide them into all truth (John 16:13). Their teaching constitutes a binding pattern for all churches (1 Corinthians 4:17; 7:17).
      3. 1 Timothy 4:16
   B. Fellowship
      1. Fellowship is association, community, joint participation, the share which one has in anything.
      2. Doctrine and fellowship are connected (Acts 2:42; 2 John 9).

3. That which was revealed by the apostles is necessary to have fellowship with them and with the Father and the Son (1 John 1:3).
      4. 1 John 1:7
   C. Breaking of bread
      1. Acts 20:7
      2. 1 Corinthians 10:16
      3. 1 Corinthians 11:23-24
   D. Prayers
      1. Colossians 4:2
      2. Acts 6:4
      3. 1 Timothy 5:5
      4. Luke 18:1
      5. 1 Thessalonians 5:17
V. Results of their continuing stedfastly
   A. Fear came upon every soul (Acts 2:43).
   B. All that believed were together (Acts 2:44).
   C. They had all things common (Acts 2:44).
   D. They sold their possessions and goods, and parted them to all, as every man had need (Acts 2:45).
   E. They continued daily with one accord in the temple (Acts 2:46).
   F. They broke bread from house to house (Acts 2:46).
   G. They ate their meat with gladness and singleness of heart (Acts 2:46).
   H. They praised God and had favor with all the people (Acts 2:47).
   I. The Lord added to the church daily (Acts 2:47).

Conclusion

1. It's not that they were baptized and end of story. They continued stedfastly!
2. May it be so of us!

~ 90 ~
When God's People Gave Too Much

Introduction

1. Upon their departure from Egypt, as the children of Israel were camped before Mount Sinai, the Lord directed His people to build the tabernacle.

    a. A portable sanctuary where God dwelled among His people to be built according to the divine pattern (Exodus 25:8-9).

    b. Exodus 25-31 records the instructions for its building.

    c. Exodus 35-40 is the account of its actual construction and erection.

    d. The materials were to be given by the Lord's people (Exodus 25:1-7).

    e. The Lord's people gave too much (Exodus 36:5-7).

2. Let's take a look at what contributed to God's people giving too much.

Discussion

I. They gave willingly

   A. A willing heart was required (Exodus 35:5; 25:2).

   B. Exodus 35:21-22, 29

   C. 2 Corinthians 8:12

II. They gave unto the Lord

   A. An offering unto the Lord (Exodus 35:5)

   B. The Lord's offering (Exodus 35:21, 24)

C. Unto the Lord (Ex. 35:22)
III. They gave to the Lord's work
   A. Exodus 35:21, 29
   B. Exodus 36:3, 5
   C. Do you know of any greater work you could give to than the Lord's work?
IV. They gave regularly
   A. "Every morning" (Exodus 36:3)
   B. 1 Corinthians 16:2
V. They gave much more than enough
   A. Exodus 36:5
   B. Restrained from bringing (Exodus 36:6-7)

Conclusion

1. Think of what God and His Son have given. Are we giving enough?
2. Why don't you give yourself to the Lord (2 Corinthians 8:5)?

~ 91 ~
Believing a Lie

Introduction

1. 2 Thessalonians 2:10-12
2. It's a sad state of affairs when men believe a lie. Let's look at some examples.

Discussion

I. Eve believed a lie
   A. Genesis 3:4-6, 13
   B. John 8:44
   C. 2 Corinthians 11:3
   D. 1 Timothy 2:14
   E. Did not release her from the penalty or consequences (Genesis 3:16, 24)

II. Isaac believed a lie
   A. Genesis 27:15-20, 24
   B. Jacob made his father believe that he was Esau to obtain the blessing (Genesis 27:35). This was a lie!
   C. Had Isaac gone by what he heard rather than what he felt, he wouldn't have been deceived!

III. Israel believed a lie
   A. Genesis 37:31-35
   B. He believed his son, Joseph, had been devoured by a wild

beast. This was a lie as his son was alive!

    C. A lie believed will produce the same feelings that would have been produced had it been true.

IV. The young prophet believed a lie

    A. 1 Kings 13:9, 11-24

    B. How sad!

V. Many today believe a lie

    A. Anything contrary to the word of God is a lie (John 17:17).

    B. Some popular lies believed today:

        1. One church is as good as another.

        2. There's no harm in a little sin.

        3. Salvation is by faith only.

        4. Baptism doesn't save.

        5. Once saved, always saved.

Conclusion

1. 1 John 4:1

2. 1 Thessalonians 5:21

~ 92 ~
Great Things in Acts Eight

Introduction

1. Acts 8 is one of the great chapters of the Bible.
2. This study brings to our attention some great things in Acts eight.

Discussion

I. Great persecution against the church

   A. Acts 8:1

   B. Jesus' teaching on persecution (Matthew 5:10-12; 23:34; John 15:20; 16:1-3).

   C. Stephen falsely accused and stoned (Acts 6:9-7:60).

   D. Saul, a driving force behind the great persecution (Acts 7:58; 8:3; 9:21; 22:4; 26:11).

   E. 2 Timothy 3:12

II. Great lamentation over Stephen

   A. Acts 8:2

   B. Prior to this, great lamentation at Herod's massacre of children (Matthew 2:16-18) and as Jesus was led to be put to death (Luke 23:27)

   C. Stephen, a great man of God (Acts 6:5, 8), was faithful unto death (Revelation 2:10).

III. Great joy in Samaria

   A. Acts 8:5-8, 12

- B. Great joy came as Christ was preached in Samaria and men and women believed and were baptized. A great message was preached with great results!
- IV. Simon gave out himself as some great one
  - A. Acts 8:9-11
  - B. Simon bewitched the people through sorcery.
  - C. Simon believed and was baptized (v. 13).
  - D. Simon sinned and was told to repent and pray (vv. 18-24).
- V. A eunuch of great authority
  - A. Acts 8:26-40
  - B. He had the charge of all the queen's treasure (v. 27).
  - C. He had come to Jerusalem to worship (v. 27).
  - D. He was reading aloud from Isaiah 53 (vv. 28-33).
  - E. He asked a question (v. 34).
  - F. He heard Jesus preached (v. 35).
  - G. He applied the sermon to himself (v. 36).
  - H. He confessed his faith (v. 37).
  - I. He stopped the chariot (v. 38).
  - J. He was baptized (v. 38).
  - K. He went on his way rejoicing (v. 39).

Conclusion

1. What a great chapter!
2. Come now as we sing.

~ 93 ~
Some Who Cannot Be Jesus' Disciple

Introduction

1. The New Testament has a lot to say about discipleship.
2. Jesus invites all to be His disciple (Matthew 11:28-30; 16:24). Yet, there are some who cannot be Jesus' disciple (Luke 14:25-33). Who cannot be Jesus' disciple?

Discussion

I. Those who do not hate family

   A. Luke 14:26

   B. The Bible teaches us to love family (Ephesians 5:25; Titus 2:4).

   C. In what sense then are we to hate family? We are to love the Lord more than family (Matthew 10:37).

   D. Following the Lord takes precedence over family relationships (Matthew 8:19-22; Luke 14:17-18, 20).

   E. Israel taught to love the Lord above family (Deuteronomy 13:6-11; Ezra 10).

   F. Abraham is a good example of one who loved the Lord above family (Genesis 22).

   G. Matthew 19:29

II. Those who do note hate their own life

   A. Luke 14:26

   B. We are to love the Lord more than we regard self (John 12:25).

    C. Some who hated their own life:
        1. Paul (Acts 20:24)
        2. Stephen (Acts 7)
        3. Epaphroditus (Philippians 2:30)
    D. There is no way we will be faithful unto death (Revelation 2:10) unless we hate our own life also!
III. Those who do not bear their cross
    A. Luke 14:27
    B. Jesus discussed counting the cost (Luke 14:28-32). Part of the cost of discipleship is cross-bearing (Luke 9:23; Matthew 10:38).
    C. Jesus bore His cross (John 19:17).
    D. Bearing the cross is being willing to suffer persecution for the cross of Christ (Galatians 6:12).
    E. Paul was a cross-bearer (Galatians 6:17).
    F. One reason some fall away is they are not willing to bear their cross (Mark 4:17).
IV. Those who do not forsake all
    A. Luke 14:33
    B. Jesus called on the rich, young, ruler to forsake all (Matthew 19:21).
    C. The disciples forsook all (Matthew 19:27; 4:18-22; Luke 5:27-28).
    D. Song: "I Surrender All"

Conclusion

1. Jesus left the Father, laid down His life, bore the cross—He forsook all!
2. Can you be Jesus' disciple? He invites! Come as we sing.

~ 94 ~
Small Things

Introduction

1. One of the great questions of the ages is, "For who hath despised the day of small things" (Zechariah 4:10)?
2. Many overlook small things. Some may look down on a thing because it's small.

Discussion

I. The Lord sometimes used small things to teach lessons of great value

    A. Proverbs 30:24-28

    B. Four little things: ants, conies, locusts, spider—exceeding wise

II. Small things often make the difference

    A. Fruit of a tree (Genesis 3:1-6)

    B. Strange fire (Leviticus 10:1-2)

    C. Smiting a rock (Numbers 20:7-12)

    D. Touching the ark (2 Samuel 6:6-7)

    E. A lie (Acts 5)

III. Small words of great importance

    A. In (1 John 5:11)

    B. If (1 Corinthians 15:1-2)

    C. And (Mark 16:16)

    D. For (Acts 2:38; Matthew 26:28)

IV. Twelve small things of the Bible

   A. A rod (Exodus 4:1-5)

   B. Manna, a small round thing (Exodus 16:14-15), bread given by God to feed His people; looked forward to Jesus, the bread of life (John 6:32-38)

   C. An ox goad (Judges 3:31), used by Shamgar to slay 600 Philistines

   D. A jawbone (Judges 15:15-17), used by Samson to slay 1,000 men

   E. A sling (1 Samuel 17:40), used by David to defeat Goliath

   F. A small remnant (Isaiah 1:9)

   G. A cup of cold water (Matthew 10:42)

   H. A grain of mustard seed (Mark 4:30-32), the smallest of seeds that grows to be the biggest of garden plants

   I. Two mites (Mark 12:41-44), constituted the greatest sacrifice of all who cast into the treasury

   J. Five barley loaves and two small fishes (John 6:5-14), fed five thousand with twelve baskets of fragments leftover

   K. A little leaven (1 Corinthians 5:6; Galatians 5:9)

   L. The tongue (James 3:4-5)

V. There is room in the kingdom for the small things you can do

   A. Song: "Room in the Kingdom"

   B. Some may think if I can't do anything big I can't do anything at all. Not so!

VI. Small number—few

   A. Saved in ark (Genesis 6-7; 1 Peter 3:20-21)

   B. Israel (Deuteronomy 7:7; 26:5)

   C. No restraint with the Lord to save by many or by few (1 Samuel 14:6); Judges 7, an example

   D. Few there be that find it (Matthew 7:13-14)

Conclusion

1. The small and great will stand before God to be judged (Revelation 20:12).
2. Are you ready?

~ 95 ~
Can Man Be Saved Without Doing Anything?

Introduction

1. Ephesians 2:8 has been misused to teach that man can do nothing to save himself. It's been said that, "man can do nothing to save himself from the consequences of his sin."

2. If it be true that man can do nothing to save himself, then man can be saved without doing anything. If not, why not?

3. It has never been true that man can do nothing to save himself.

Discussion

I. Noah was not saved without doing anything

    A. Hebrews 11:7; 1 Peter 3:20

    B. Genesis 6

II. Rahab was not saved without doing anything

    A. Joshua 6:25

    B. Bind line of scarlet thread, stay in the house, keep quiet (Joshua 2:6, 15, 18-20)

III. Those on Pentecost were not saved without doing anything

    A. Acts 2:37-38

    B. Watch verse 40!

IV. Saul was not saved without doing anything

    A. Acts 9:6; 22:10

B. Acts 22:16
V. Cornelius was not saved without doing anything
　　A. "What thou oughtest to do" (Acts 10:6)
　　B. Acts 11:14
VI. The Philippian jailor was not saved without doing anything
　　A. Acts 16:30-31
　　B. Note what he did (vv. 32-34).

Conclusion

1. There are two sides to salvation: grace (God's) and faith (man's).
2. Hebrews 5:9

~ 96 ~
The Home at the Beginning

Introduction

1. Matthew 19:4-6

2. We need to be brought back to the home at the beginning (Genesis 1-2).

Discussion

I. A divine home

   A. It was God who, in the beginning, created the heaven and the earth (Genesis 1:1).

   B. It was God who formed man of the dust of the ground (Genesis 2:7).

   C. It was God who said, "It is not good that the man should be alone; I will make him an help meet for him" (Genesis 2:18).

   D. It was God who caused a deep sleep to fall upon Adam (Genesis 2:21).

   E. It was God who took one of his ribs and closed up the flesh instead thereof (Genesis 2:21).

   F. It was God who with the rib which he had taken from man made a woman (Genesis 2:22).

   G. It was God who brought her unto the man (Genesis 2:22).

   H. Jesus said, "What God hath joined together, let not man put asunder" (Matthew 19:6).

96. The Home at the Beginning

I. The home originated with God! We need to respect His rules governing it.

II. A companionship-providing home

   A. Genesis 2:18

   B. Man needed a companion. God provided man's need of companionship in the home. He made one just right for him (Genesis 2:22).

III. A male and female home

   A. Matthew 19:4

   B. The beasts of the field were unsuitable (Genesis 2:19-20; Leviticus 20:15-16).

   C. It was not a male and male arrangement, nor a female and female affair (Leviticus 18:22; 20:13; Jude 7; Genesis 19; Romans 1:21-32).

   D. It was not a man and his wives (Genesis 2:24-25).

   E. It was not a live-in affair, but a marriage relationship (Genesis 2:24; Mark 10:6-8).

IV. A stable home

   A. Many homes today aren't very stable.

   B. God designed the home at the beginning to endure.

      1. "Leave" and "cleave"—permanence (Genesis 2:24)

      2. The home at the beginning knew nothing about divorce (Matthew 19:8).

V. A husband-headed home

   A. Genesis 3:16

   B. 1 Timothy 2:12-14

   C. 1 Corinthians 11:3

   D. Ephesians 5:22-24

VI. A child-rearing home

   A. Genesis 1:28

- B. The home is the place to have and rear children (Genesis 4:1-2, 25).
- C. About 40% of children in America are born out of wedlock each year. Don't get the carriage before the marriage! (1 Corinthians 6:18; 7:1-2).
- D. Children need to be trained (Proverbs 22:6; 29:15, 17; Ephesians 6:4).

Conclusion

1. Hebrews 13:4
2. Society would be much improved if we restore the home as God designed it at the beginning.
3. We invite you to become married to Christ (Romans 7:4).

~ 97 ~
David's Temple Preparations

Introduction

1. It came into David's mind to build a house for God, but God had other plans. God had plans of building David a house, and his son, Solomon, building a house for His name (2 Samuel 7:1-17).

2. There are some things that stand out about David from a reading of 2 Samuel 7; 1 Chronicles 22; 28-29. Thus, we study.

Discussion

I. David's humility

  A. "Who am I, O Lord God? and what is my house, that thou hast brought me hitherto" (2 Samuel 7:18)?

  B. Contrast with King Uzziah who became wroth and acted presumptuously (2 Chronicles 26:16-21).

  C. We are to be "clothed with humility" (1 Peter 5:5-6).

II. David's respect for the Lord's word

  A. Several times David makes mention of the Lord's word:

    1. "thou hast spoken" (v. 19)

    2. "thy word's sake" (v. 21)

    3. "the word that thou hast spoken" (v. 25)

    4. "hast revealed to thy servant, saying" (v. 27)

    5. "thy words" (v. 28)

    6. "God, hast spoken" (v. 29)

7. "the word of the Lord came to me, saying" (1 Chronicles 22:8)

8. "God said unto me" (1 Chronicles 28:3)

9. "And he said unto me" (1 Chronicles 28:6)

B. David was content with the Lord's word—"establish it for ever, and do as thou hast said" (v. 25).

C. David recognized the truthfulness of the Lord's word—"thy words be true" (v. 28).

III. David's attitude toward the Lord and His people

A. Notice David's attitude toward the Lord (v. 22).

B. Observe David's attitude toward the Lord's people (vv. 23-24).

IV. David's exhortation to his brethren and his son

A. David's exhortation to his son, Solomon (1 Chronicles 22:6-16; 28:9-21)

1. The Lord be with thee (22:11).

2. Keep the law of the Lord (22:12).

3. Be strong, and of good courage; dread not, nor be dismayed (22:13).

4. Arise, and be doing (22:16).

5. Note David's exhortation to Solomon in 1 Chronicles 28:9, 20.

B. David's exhortation to his brethren (1 Chronicles 22:17-19; 28:1-8)

V. David's giving Solomon the pattern

A. Anytime God has instructed man to build, He has given him a pattern by which to build.

1. The ark (Genesis 6:14-15)

2. The tabernacle (Exodus 25:8-9; Hebrews 8:5)

B. True also of the temple (1 Chronicles 28:11-19). Observe the use of the word "pattern" (vv. 11, 12, 18, 19).

1. The pattern was "by the spirit" (v. 12).

2. The pattern was made to be understood (v. 19).

VI. David's disposition toward the temple building

  A. "The house that is to be builded for the Lord must be exceeding magnifical, of fame and of glory throughout all countries" (1 Chronicles 22:5).

  B. "The work is great: for the palace is not for man, but for the Lord God" (1 Chronicles 29:1).

  C. David's disposition led him to make preparations for the building of the temple (1 Chronicles 22:5-6).

    1. He "prepared abundantly before his death" (22:5).

    2. He "prepared with all his might" (29:2).

    3. He "set masons to hew wrought stones to build the house of God" (22:2), "prepared iron in abundance for the nails" (22:3), "brass in abundance without weight" (22:3), "cedar trees in abundance" (22:4), "an hundred thousand talents of gold, and a thousand thousand talents of silver; and of brass and iron without weight; for it is in abundance: timber also and stone" (22:14), "workmen...in abundance" (22:15).

VII. David's affection to the house of God

  A. Matthew 6:19-21

  B. This is illustrated in King David. His heart was to the house of God, and that's where his treasure was (1 Chronicles 29:3-5).

  C. This influenced others to give willingly for the service of the house of God (1 Chronicles 29:5-22). They gave so freely and abundantly because they recognized they were giving God what was His (vv. 14, 16).

  D. "Set your affection on things above, not on things on the earth" (Colossians 3:2).

Conclusion

1. One reason it could be said that the house was finished throughout all the parts thereof, and according to all the fashion of it (1 Kings 6:38) is because of David's preparations for it!

2. Let's be like David when it comes to the church (1 Timothy 3:15).

~ 98 ~
Anna

Introduction

1. Luke 2:36-38

    a. The setting: Luke tells of the birth of Jesus. Joseph and Mary take the child to Jerusalem to present him to the Lord according to the law of Moses. At this temple scene, we meet two outstanding people: Simeon and Anna.

    b. This is the only time Anna is mentioned in the Bible. Her name means "grace."

2. Let's observe some things said about this first-century woman.

Discussion

I. A prophetess

    A. Verse 36

    B. She was a female prophet, inspired to speak the word of God.

    C. Other prophetesses mentioned: Miriam (Exodus 15:20), Deborah (Judges 4:4), Huldah (2 Kings 22:14), Noadiah (Nehemiah 6:14), and Isaiah's wife (Isaiah 8:3)

    D. There were women in New Testament days who prophesied (Joel 2:28-29; Acts 21:8-9; 1 Corinthians 11:5).

    E. No prophets or prophetesses today (1 Corinthians 12:10; 13:8-13).

II. Of a great age

    A. Verse 36

B. We need to know how to treat those who are older (Leviticus 19:32; 1 Timothy 5:1-2; 1 Peter 5:5).

C. Titus 2:3-4 points out some responsibilities of aged women.

III. Lived with a husband

A. Verse 36

B. God arranged this relationship at the beginning (Genesis 2:18-24; Matthew 19:4-6).

C. This is a life-long living (Matthew 19:6; Romans 7:2-3; 1 Corinthians 7:39).

D. The role of the woman living with a husband (Genesis 3:16; 1 Corinthians 7:3-4; Ephesians 5:22-33; Colossians 3:18; Titus 2:4-5; 1 Peter 3:1-6).

E. "From her virginity" indicates she avoided fornication (1 Corinthians 7:2).

IV. A widow

A. Verse 37

B. One who has lost her husband by death and has not remarried.

C. God has always provided for widows (Deuteronomy 14:28-29; 24:19-20).

D. New Testament teaching concerning widows (Acts 6:1; 1 Timothy 5:3-16; James 1:27).

V. Departed not from the temple

A. Verse 37

B. If you had been Anna, would folks have expected to see you at the temple?

VI. Served God night and day

A. Verse 37

B. She was constant and regular, stedfast and faithful!

C. One of the qualifications of a widow indeed (1 Timothy 5:5).

D. Teaching concerning prayer (Matthew 6:5-15) and fasting (Matthew 6:16-18).

VII. Gave thanks unto the Lord

    A. Verse 38

    B. We ought to give thanks unto the Lord (Ephesians 5:20).

    C. We have so much to be thankful for!

VIII. Spoke of Him

    A. Verse 38

    B. She spoke to others about the Lord!

    C. Redemption, the forgiveness of sins (Ephesians 1:7), is in Christ (Romans 3:24).

Conclusion

1. What a remarkable woman!
2. Be an Anna!

~ 99 ~
This One Thing I Do

Introduction

1. Philippians 3:13-14
2. The Scriptures put emphasis on one thing:
   a. Mark 10:21
   b. Luke 10:42
   c. John 9:25
   d. 2 Peter 3:8
   e. Philippians 3:13
3. In this study, we notice the one thing Paul did, how he did it, why he did it, and the fact that we must do it too.

Discussion

I. What he did
   A. Philippians 3:14
   B. He pressed for the prize.
      1. He pressed as one who in a race runs swiftly to reach the goal.
      2. For the prize: He was not working for a garland of leaves, a silver cup, or a gold medal. He was striving for an incorruptible crown (1 Corinthians 9:24-27).

II. How he did it
   A. Philippians 3:13

B. Two things involved:
   1. Forgetting those things which are behind
      a. Past failures and mistakes (1 Timothy 1:15; Acts 7:58; 8:1, 3; Luke 9:62)
      b. Past accomplishments and achievements: He did not boast as though he had done enough. Some reach a point where they think they've done enough and spend the rest of their lives doing very little in the Lord's service.
   2. Reaching forth unto those things which are before
      a. He was like an athlete straining forward to what lies ahead.
      b. He would not relax his effort to reach his goal.

III. Why he did it
   A. Philippians 3:11-13
   B. He had not yet taken hold of the ultimate prize. He was still in the flesh and had not yet attained the heavenly goal. Thus, he continued to put forth strenuous effort to win the prize.
   C. Some act as if they have already won the prize!

IV. We must do it too
   A. Philippians 3:15-21
   B. Paul is an example to mark, keep your eye on, as worthy of following.
   C. Don't serve your own selfish desires; don't be fixed upon the things of this present life.
      1. To live is Christ, to die is gain (Philippians 1:21).
      2. Christ liveth in me (Galatians 2:20).
      3. Christ is our life (Colossians 3:4).
   D. Stay focused on heaven. When Christ comes, our salvation will be complete!

Conclusion

1. May we live our lives as Paul with a singular focus on Christ.
2. Will we gain other things and lose Christ or give up everything to win Him?

~ 100 ~
People of the Book

Introduction

1. God has put His words in a book, and expects His people to be people of the book.

    a. Deuteronomy 17:18-20

    b. Deuteronomy 28:58

    c. Deuteronomy 30:10

    d. Joshua 1:8

    e. Joshua 23:6

2. This study challenges us to be people of the book.

Discussion

I. Some people of the book

   A. The children of Israel (Exodus 24:3-8)

   B. Amaziah (2 Kings 14:1-6; Deuteronomy 24:16)

   C. Josiah (2 Kings 22-23)

   D. The people before the water gate (Nehemiah 8)

      1. They asked for the book (v. 1).

      2. They were attentive unto the book (v. 3).

      3. They made provisions for the reading of the book (v. 4).

      4. They stood up for the book (v. 5).

      5. They wept over the book (v. 9).

       6. They made application of the book (vv. 14-17).

II. Characteristics of people of the book
- A. They know the book.
    1. There's no substitute for knowing the book (John 8:32).
    2. There's no excuse for ignorance (Hosea 4:6).
    3. Some things we can do to better know the book:
        a. Desire to be taught it (Psalm 25:4-5; Acts 8:31).
        b. Ask questions (Acts 8:34).
        c. Read and study it (Ephesians 3:4; 2 Timothy 2:15; 1 Timothy 4:13; Revelation 1:3).
- B. They live the book.
    1. We must do (Matthew 7:21, 24-27; John 9:31; James 1:22, 25; Revelation 22:14).
    2. Able to say, "Follow me, as I follow Christ" (1 Corinthians 11:1).
- C. They teach the book.
    1. Share it with others (Acts 8:4; 2 Timothy 2:2).
    2. Be an Ezra (Ezra 7:10).

Conclusion

1. In past generations, members of the church of Christ were viewed as walking Bibles.
2. May we be people of the book!

www.ingramcontent.com/pod-product-compliance
Lightning Source LLC
Chambersburg PA
CBHW070610170426
43200CB00012B/2646